In 1945 Qatar had no schools or telephones and only one doctor to serve the estimated population of around 25,000. During the 1950s and 1960s the economy grew as oil revenues poured in. By the mid-1970s Qatar had the second highest GNP per head in the world, exceeded only by Kuwait.

The evolution of the monetary and banking system in Qatar enabling this transformation has not, until now, been well documented.

This book chronicles the abandonment of the Gulf rupee as the official currency and the adoption of the Qatari riyal, the creation of a currency board followed by the Qatar Monetary Agency and ultimately the creation of a central bank.

The text draws uniquely on statistical analysis drawn from the official archives and from the British Embassy for the time period.

The author was formerly an advisor to the CEO of a branch of the Islamic Development Bank Group in Saudi Arabia and previously Chief Economist at the Central Bank of Bahrain.

Dedication

This book is dedicated to my wife Nadia, who keeps the ship afloat, my son Alexei who is embarking on a new exciting stage in his life and whose Excel skills have saved my life and my little treasure, my daughter Anna.

THE MONEY AND BANKING HISTORY OF QATAR

ISBN: 978-1-7398004-0-6

The Money and Banking History of the Middle East Series

Series Author: Brian Kettell

Brian Kettell has lived and worked in the Middle East for more than 20 years. Most recently he worked as an advisor to the CEO of a branch of the Islamic Development Bank in Jeddah, Saudi Arabia. Prior to that he was Economic Advisor for the Central Bank of Bahrain where he had numerous economics and banking responsibilities. He has taught at several universities in the Middle East.

1. The Money and Banking History of the United Arab Emirates
2. The Money and Banking History of Bahrain
3. The Money and Banking History of Qatar
4. The Money and Banking History of Kuwait
5. The Money and Banking History of Oman
6. The Money and Banking History of Iraq
7. The Money and Banking History of Libya
8. The Money and Banking History of Jordan
9. The Money and Banking History of Palestine
10. The Money and Banking History of North and South Yemen
11. The Money and Banking History of Saudi Arabia.

Qatar is the third book in the series.

Contents

Chapter 1. The History of Qatar	Where is Qatar? Early history. The Al Thani family. Role of the British in Qatar. Qatar as a dependency of Bahrain.
Chapter 2. The Discovery of Oil and its Impact on Qatar	Discovery of Oil in Qatar. Petroleum production, refining and exports. Government revenues from oil. Natural gas finds. Impact of oil discoveries on the economy. Industrialisation begins.
Chapter 3. Monetary environment in the Middle East and the Gulf	Early origins of the Qatari currency. Qatar and the Sterling Area. Currency arrangements prior to the introduction of the Qatari dinar. Breakdown of the Sterling Area. Emergence of Gulf currency boards and the issue of currencies.
Chapter 4. Currency Boards: Predecessors of Central Banks	What is an Orthodox Currency Board? Currency Board Principles. Why were they created and how do they differ from central banks?
Appendix 4.1	Currency Board Principles by C.E. Loombe.
Appendix 4.2 Sterilisation Coefficients	
Chapter 5. Creation of the Qatar-Dubai Currency Board and the Qatar Monetary Agency	Creation of the Qatar-Dubai Currency Board and the Qatar Monetary Agency. Was the Qatar Currency Board a success? Currency Board Analysis: Testing for Currency Board Orthodoxy.
Appendix 5.1	The Qatar Dubai-Currency Authority. (QDCA). The Creation of the Qatar-Currency Board

Appendix 5.2	Qatar and Dubai Currency Board Financial Statements.
Appendix 5.3	Annual reports of the Qatar and Dubai Currency Board.
Appendix 5.4	Authorised Currency Backing and Orthodoxy Tests.
Appendix 5.5	The Qatar Monetary Agency Law.
Chapter 6. The Monetary and Banking Environment within Qatar and its impact on Commercial Banking	Commercial Banking during the Currency Board Period. Monetary and economic factors affecting the growth of commercial banks.
Appendix 6.1	Consolidated balance sheets of commercial banks in Qatar, 1965-1972
Appendix 1	Currency arrangements in the Gulf States prior to the formation of Central Banks.
Appendix 2	Currency Arrangements in the Middle East (the Gulf States) prior to IMF membership.
Appendix 3	From Currency Board (Monetary Agency) to IMF membership: The Gulf States
Appendix 4	From Currency Board (Currency Commission) to IMF Membership: The Middle East (excluding the Gulf States)

Chapter 1

Qatar: From Pearl Diving to Regional Powerhouse

Where is Qatar?

The state of Qatar occupies a peninsula (roughly 160 kilometres long, and between 55 km and 90 km wide), projecting northwards from the Arabian mainland, on the west coast of the Persian Gulf. Its western coastline joins onto the shores of Saudi Arabia, and to the east lies the United Arab Emirates and Oman. The total area of Qatar is 11,437 sq km (4,416 sq miles).

Qatar's landward frontiers, at the neck of the peninsula, are shared with Saudi Arabia to the west and Abu Dhabi to the east, while the nearest seaward neighbours are Bahrain and Saudi Arabia.

Early history [1,2]

Human occupation of Qatar dates back 50,000 years. Stone Age encampments and tools have been unearthed in the peninsula. Mesopotamia was the first civilisation to have a presence in the area during the Neolithic period, evidenced by the discovery of potsherds originating from the Ubaid period found near coastal encampments.

The peninsula fell under the domain of several different empires during its early years of settlement, including the Seleucid, the Parthians and the Sasanians.

In 628 AD, the population was introduced to Islam after Muhammad sent an envoy to Munzir ibn Sawa, the Sasanid governor of eastern Arabia. It became a pearl trading centre by the 8th century. The Abbasid era saw the rise of several settlements.

After the Bani Utbah and other Arab tribes conquered Bahrain in 1783, the Al Khalifa imposed their authority over Bahrain and mainland Qatar. Over the preceding centuries, Qatar was a site of contention between the Wahhabi of Najd and the Al Khalifa tribe. The Ottomans expanded their empire into eastern Arabia in 1871 although withdrawing from the area in 1915, after the beginning of World War I. In 1945 the country had no schools or telephones, and only one doctor to serve the estimated population of around 25,000, of whom about a fifth lived in the capital, Doha.

During the 1950s and 1960s the economy grew as oil revenues poured in, although development was limited until the accession of Sheikh Khalifa bin Hamad in 1972.

By the mid-1970s Qatar had the second highest GNP per head in the world, exceeded only by Kuwait.

Qatari history has been heavily influenced by its links to Bahrain. Qatari Bahraini ties can be explained by a period of dominance over Qatar by the Khalifa family of Bahrain. This ended with the Turkish occupation in 1872.

Qatar's ties with Saudi Arabia were based on religion as the ruling families, in both countries, belonged to the Wahhabi sect of Islam.

During the middle and late 18th century a branch of the Utub tribe in Kuwait, known as the Al-Khalifa, emigrated to Qatar, and eventually settled on the northwest coast of the peninsula. The Al-Khalifa tribe had a long-established reputation as accomplished sailors and skilled traders and this soon became the mainstay of commercial development in the region of Qatar.

The Qatar peninsula became part of Turkey's Ottoman empire in 1872, but Turkish forces evacuated Qatar at the beginning of World War I.

The United Kingdom recognised Sheikh Abdullah bin Jassim Al Thani as Emir of Qatar, and in 1916 made a treaty with him. This was in line with its policy in Bahrain, the Trucial States (which later became the United Arab Emirates) and Kuwait.

The Emir of Qatar undertook not to cede, mortgage, or otherwise dispose of parts of his territories to anyone except the British Government, nor to enter any relationship with a foreign government, other than the British, without British consent.

In return, Britain undertook to protect Qatar from aggression by sea, and to provide support in case of an overland attack. A further treaty, concluded in 1934, extended British protection to Qatar.

Prior to the discovery of oil, the Qataris earned their livelihood by herding in the desert and, in the coastal areas, by fishing and pearling.

Like the other sheikhdoms around the western coast of the Gulf, Qatar was a centre for the pearl industry. The decline of this industry in the 1930s, due mainly to Japan's development of cultured pearls, threatened this limited but vital source of income and employment for most of the population.

The discovery of oil and the beginning of production brought Qatar the revenues and employment the economy needed at a most opportune time. In December 1949, Qatar became an exporter of crude oil, with its first shipment to Europe.

This event marks the beginning of what, by the beginning of the 20th century, led to Qatar, on a per capita basis, to being the richest country in the world.

In October 1960, Sheikh Ali bin Abdullah Al Thani, who had been Emir of Qatar since 1949, abdicated in favour of his son, Sheikh Ahmad bin Ali Al Thani.

In 1968 the British Government announced its intention to withdraw British forces from the Arabian Gulf by 1971. As a result, Qatar attempted to associate itself with Bahrain and the Trucial States in a proposed federation.

In April 1970 the Emir, Sheikh Ahmad, announced a provisional constitution for Qatar, providing for a partially elected consultative assembly. Effective power remained, however, in the monarch's hands. In May 1970 the Deputy Emir Sheikh Khalifa Al Thani (a cousin of Sheikh Ahmad), was appointed Prime Minister.

After the failure of negotiations for union with neighbouring Gulf countries, Qatar became fully independent on 1 September 1971, when the ruler took the title of Emir. The 1916 treaty was replaced by a new treaty of friendship with the United Kingdom.

In February 1972 a bloodless coup, led by Sheikh Khalifa, the Crown prince and Prime Minister, deposed the Emir during his absence abroad. Claiming support from the royal family and the armed forces, Sheikh Khalifa proclaimed himself emir and claimed the title.

The British relationship with Qatar

Many external influences contributed to the early development of Qatar's statehood. By the early 19th century, the influence of the conservative Wahhabi sect had spread from the Arabian Desert to the Gulf.

In fact, the British, as the only European power in the region at the time, sought to bring a measure of control to the unstructured, free-moving sea traffic of the Gulf through the colonial government in Bombay.

By 1820 the British had persuaded the Arab sheikhs on the then so-called Pirate Coast to sign the General Maritime Treaty signed to outlaw warfare during the all-important pearl diving season. The truce was renewed every year until the Perpetual Maritime Truce was signed in 1853. The term Trucial Coast was derived from the series of truces signed by the sheikhdoms along the western coastline of the Gulf to the south of Kuwait.

British interest in maintaining stability in the region stemmed from a desire to protect the shipping lanes of the Gulf to the Indian sub-continent. Oil was decades away from being discovered in the Arabian Peninsula.

It was during the mid-19th century that the burgeoning power of the Al Thani family began to be felt. The Al Thanis had emigrated from Central Arabia to settle around Doha, the modern day capital of Qatar.

On 12 September 1868 a treaty was signed by Muhammad bin Thani and the British Political Resident, Lieutenant Colonel Lewis Pelly, to outlaw war at sea and to refer any conflict to the British Resident of the region. This treaty was like other trucial pacts concluded with the British by the neighbouring sheikhdoms.

This period in Qatar's history continued to be somewhat stormy. The Ottoman Turks had since moved into the Gulf region and effectively controlled the port city of Doha. However, the Al Thani family waited to assert themselves once again as the *de facto* rulers of Qatar.

In 1879 Muhammad bin Thani's son Sheikh Jasim was appointed Governor of Qatar by the Turks in Doha. In March 1893, Sheikh Jasim seized the opportunity to score a rousing victory over the Turks, although their influence was not totally eradicated.

In July 1913, Sheikh Jasim died and was succeeded by his son Abdullah whose crowning achievement was to complete the treaty of November 1916 with the British to become part of the Trucial system.

The Gulf had assumed increasing importance as the main sea route to India and the Far East since the latter part of the 16th century. It had been long considered the principal trading route between the east and west.

Qatar's strategic position on the Gulf had attracted British attention. Interested in safeguarding the sea route to India throughout the 19th century and the early years of the 1900s, Britain pursued a policy of containing the Ottoman presence and influence on the western shores of the Gulf.

This policy culminated in the 1916 Treaty, noted above, and the expulsion of the Turkish garrison from Doha.

The treaty was essentially like the arrangements concluded with Bahrain, Kuwait, and the Trucial sheikhdoms. Among the features of these treaties, which expanded and continued the British influence in the Gulf until the 1970s, was that the Foreign Office in London would handle the protectorates' foreign relations.

The discovery of petroleum in 1939 promised greater prosperity for Qatar, but further development was delayed by the onset of World War Two and production did not begin on a commercial scale until 1949. See Chapter 2 for more discussion of this.

Qatar used the revenues from the export of petroleum to finance an ambitious development programme.

In January 1961 Qatar joined the Organisation of the Petroleum Exporting Countries (OPEC).

The Treaty of Protection between Great Britain and Qatar lasted until 1 September 1971 when Qatar was declared an independent state under Sheikh Khalifa bin Hamad Al Thani. The two states signed a Treaty of Friendship only days later, which called for mutual consultation on matters of common concern. This marked the termination of several other treaty relationships of various forms which had existed with the United Kingdom since 1896.

On 11 September 1971, Qatar was admitted to the League of Arab States. Five days later, the Security Council of the United Nations unanimously recommended Qatar's acceptance followed by ratification, on 21 September of that year, by the General Assembly.

The United Arab Emirates (Abu Dhabi, Ajman, Dubai, Fujairah, Sharjah, Umm al-Qaiwain) formed in 1971 an independent country. Ras al-Khaimah joined in 1972.

Bahrain and Qatar opted for separate independence.

Qatar had no constitution until the new provisional constitution was announced on 2 April 1970, to become effective that July, making it the first of the Gulf sheikhdoms to adopt such a written document of government. Prior to that announcement all the powers of government were vested in the Emir, the ruler of Qatar.

SELECTED REFERENCES

[1] El Mallakh, Ragaei. *Qatar: Development of an Oil Economy.* Croom Helm, London and St Martin's Press, New York 1979

[2] El Mallakh, Ragaei. *Qatar: Energy and Development.* Croom Helm, London and St Martin's Press, New York 1985.

Nafi, Zuhair Ahmed. *Economic and Social Development in Qatar.* Frances Pinter, London and Dover, New Hampshire 1983

Sadik, Muhammed T. and Snavely, William P. *Bahrain, Qatar, and the United Arab Emirates.* D.C. Heath and Company, Lexington, Mass. 1972

Graham, Helga. *Arabian Time Machine: Self-Portrait of an Oil State.* Heinemann, London 1978.

Chapter 2

The Discovery of Oil and Gas and its impact on Qatar during the Currency Board period

Before the emergence of its petrol-based industry, Qatar was a poor economy largely based on pearl diving. The exploration of oil and gas fields began in 1939. In 1973, oil production and revenues increased dramatically, moving Qatar out of the ranks of the world's poorest countries and providing it with one of the highest per capita incomes in the world.

In January 1940 with the discovery of the onshore Dukhan Field, Qatar joined the Middle East's oil club. In 1960 Qatar's first offshore field was discovered.

As early as 1922, Major Frank Holmes (also called Abu Naft or Father of Oil in the Middle East) had his eye on Qatar's oil resources. Holmes was a New Zealand-born British miner, army officer and oil businessman who represented the London-based Eastern and General Syndicate's ventures in the Middle East. He helped obtain oil concessions in Saudi Arabia, Kuwait and Bahrain in the 1920s

Holmes negotiated with Qatar's ruler Sheikh Abdullah bin Jassim Al Thani in Doha in 1923. However, this venture did not proceed given that the British Colonial Office had prohibited oil ventures in Qatar.

By 1925, however, such restrictions appear to have eased for, in early 1926, George Martin Lees, a geologist with the Anglo-Persian Oil Company (APOC), later British Petroleum, visited Doha and made a one-day trip to a few outcrops of Qatar. These he identified as Eocene limestone exposed on the crest of a gently dipping anticline, potentially a source for oil to be found.

Before leaving, Lees also obtained permission from the sheikh to explore the emirate for the next two years.

What renewed the British interest in Qatar's oil was the 1932 discovery of oil in Bahrain by Socal, the Standard Oil Company of California. Alarmed by the American company's success in the region, APOC sent Charles Mylles to Doha to negotiate an oil concession with the sheikh. In August 1932, APOC was granted a two-year exploration license in Qatar.

This venture, however, posed a problem for APOC as the company had signed the 1928 Red Line Agreement with a consortium of oil companies known as the Iraq Petroleum Company (IPC) to the effect that no member of the consortium would be engaged, on its own, in any exploration activity in the former Ottoman empire of the Middle East.

Qatar was included in the Red Line Agreement. APOC informed IPC of its option in Qatar, and IPC permitted APOC to act as its nominee in Qatar.

Late in 1932, APOC dispatched two geologists, E.W. Shaw and P.T. Cox, to Qatar. After a survey during January-March 1933, the team found that the Dukhan anticline in south eastern Qatar shared similarities with the discovery field in Bahrain. Its surface rocks were Eocene limestone and hence good potential for a Cretaceous reservoir rock (like that of Bahrain).

In 1933-34, APOC dispatched W.E. Browne to map the Dukhan anticline. After this mapping, APOC entered a negotiation with Qatar, and on 17 May 1935, it was granted a 75-year oil concession, covering all of Qatar's land, to explore, find and produce oil.

In return, the Qatar government was to receive a royalty of 2 Indian rupees per ton of oil produced, a payment of Rs. 400,000 on signature, and annual sums of Rs. 150,000 (after five years, Rs. 300,000) in addition to the royalty.

This date marked the beginning of Qatar becoming an oil and, later, gas rich economy. Two years later APOC, on behalf of IPC, created a new company called Petroleum Department of Qatar, which took over the concession and its operations. This new company included BP (23.75%), Royal Dutch Shell (23.75%), Cie Francaise des Petroles (23.75%), Standard Oil of New Jersey (11.87%), Mobil (11.87%), and Paratex (Gulbenkian Foundation) (5%).

During the winter of 1937-38 a new group of geologists, Norval E. Baker, T.F. Williamson, and R. Pomeyrol, visited Dukhan to locate a drilling site. They examined the Dukhan anticline, which was 80 km long with 90 metres of structural closure in the Middle Eocene limestone, and recommended a location for the first well.

Onshore and Offshore Concessions

After World War I and the collapse of the Ottoman Empire, Qatar fell within the British sphere of influence. The first onshore oil concession in the country was awarded in 1935 to British Petroleum's predecessor, the Anglo-Iranian Oil Company (AIOC). Because of its obligations under the Red Line Agreement, AIOC transferred the concession to an associate company of the Iraq Petroleum Co., Petroleum Development (Qatar) Ltd (PDQ), which would operate the concession.

PDQ was later renamed the Qatar Petroleum Company (QPC). In October 1938 Dukhan No. 1 was spudded and yielded 4,000 barrels per day (640 m^3/d) by January 1940. However World War Two delayed development until 1947. The first crude exports occurred in 1949.

The first offshore concessions were granted in 1949 to the International Marine Oil Company (IMOC), which was a subsidiary of Superior Oil and the London-registered Central Mining & Investment Company. In 1952, after IMOC had withdrawn, the Shell Company Qatar (SCQ) acquired exploration rights to most of the offshore territory. In 1960 and 1963, the Idd Al-Shargi and Maydan Mahzam fields were discovered respectively. The largest offshore field, Bul Hanine, was discovered in 1970 and came onstream in 1972.

Crude oil production began in 1949 with a minimal 730,000 barrels for the year. It increased steadily through to the mid-1970s. Until mid-1984 the maximum annual production had been in 1973 when liftings had averaged some 570,000 bpd.

As can be seen from Figure 2.1 crude petroleum production grew rapidly from 1966 to 1973, the currency board period.

Figure 2.1 Qatar Crude Petroleum Production 1966-1972

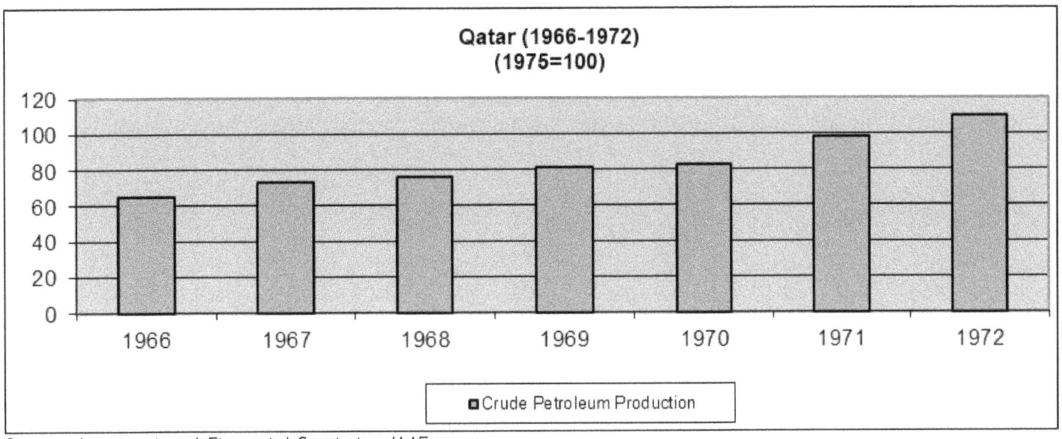

Source: International Financial Statistics, IMF

Until the early 1980s virtually all crude oil was exported, with the effect that export earnings, the balance of payments, and government spending reflected the fluctuations in production. Exports peaked in 1973, when Qatar exported more than 200 million barrels of crude oil.

Figure 2.2 highlights that export prices of crude petroleum grew dramatically, particularly in the latter years of the currency board period.

Figure 2.2 Export Price of Crude Petroleum 1966-1972

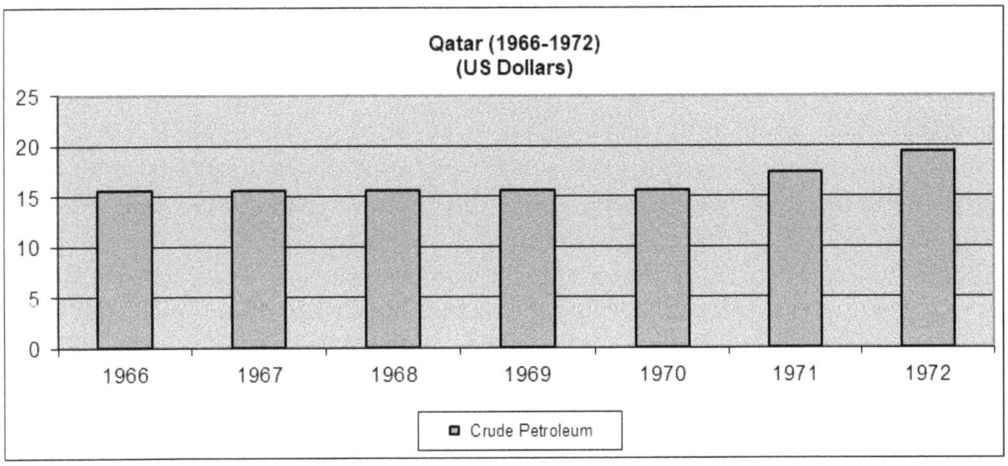

Source: International Financial Statistics, IMF

Crude petroleum exports also grew dramatically during the currency board period. See Figure 2.3.

Figure 2.3 International Transactions 1966-1972

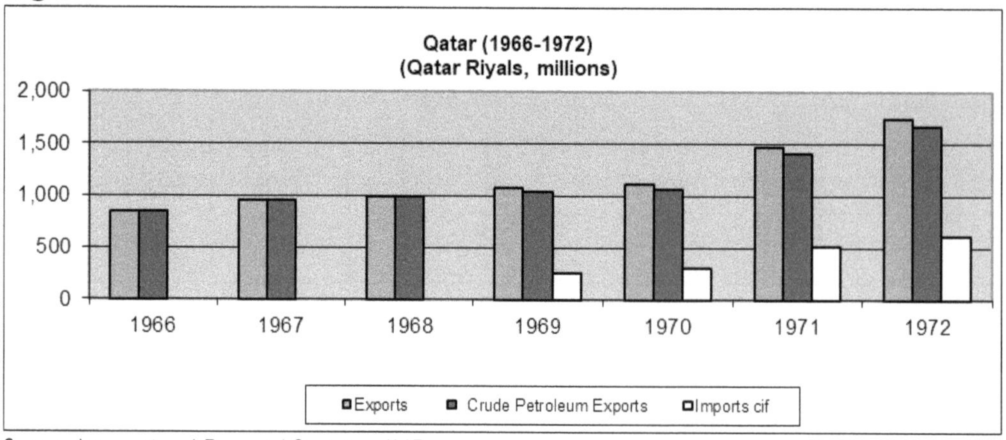

Source: International Financial Statistics, IMF

Industrialisation begins in Qatar

Industrialisation in Qatar began, as one might expect, only after the discovery and exploitation of the country's oil resources. Growth of the manufacturing sector moved slowly at first because roads, ports utilities, and other infrastructure needs were lacking.

The small indigenous labour force was uneducated and unskilled. There were constant efforts at Qatarisation of the work force, and the number of Qatari's in management and skilled positions expanded over the years. Nonetheless, most of the labour force for both technical and menial work was expatriate.

In the mid-1980s an effort to Arabise the labour force - to substitute Arabs for the large number of Asian and South Asian workers - was added to the drive for Qatarisation.

Industrialisation faced further obstacles in that the domestic market was negligible. Most manufacturing was, of necessity, oriented to the export market where there were already established competitors. The government actively encouraged industrial and manufacturing projects in order to diversify the basis of the economy and make the best use of Qatar's natural resources.

Oil revenues provided the capital to finance infrastructure and capitalise on several large scale oil related industries.

Natural gas resources provided a relatively cheap source of power. Gas was used as the direct reductions agent in the iron and steel industry. It provided feedstock for the petrochemical industries producing nitrogenous fertilisers, ethylene, and a variety of by-products.

Cheap power gave Qatari industry a competitive edge in fields dominated by more established industries. The government followed a strategy of import substitution, looking for capital intensive industries with low labour requirements to limit the need to import foreign workers.

Budgetary surpluses and oil revenue

Oil revenues made up the bulk of government receipts, and government spending was the primary means of injecting oil earnings into the local economy. See Figure 2.3. Given the small size of the local market, government spending generated most of the domestic economic activity.

Following the lead of other oil-rich Gulf states, Qatar's budget funded health, education, housing and a number of other social welfare programmes. These were designed to improve living conditions and increase the number of Qatari's trained to play technical and managerial roles in oil and other industries.

There was also extensive spending to establish the country's infrastructure and to diversify the economy against the time when Qatar's oil reserves became depleted.

The government built roads, upgraded port facilities, and constructed power and desalination plants. There were massive outlays on industrial plants in the mid to late 1970s.

Government budgets followed an expansionary policy from 1974 to 1977. In an effort to build infrastructure the government pumped a large portion of the increases from the 1973 hike in oil prices into costly, large-scale projects and underwrote a plethora of social welfare programmes. Citizens received free education, health care, electricity and water. The government invested massive amounts in school buildings, land reclamation, industrial plants and equipment and utilities.

Qatar joined the Organisation of Petroleum Exporting Countries (OPEC) in January 1961, soon after the organisation's founding. The country has been a member of the Organisation of Arab Petroleum Exporting Countries (OAPEC) since mid-1970.

Nationalisation of the oil sector

In 1973, the state acquired a 25 per cent stake in the onshore concessions of QPC and offshore concessions of SCQ. As part of the agreement, the government stake would increase by 5 per cent every year until it reached 51 percent in 1981. However, in early 1974, the initial agreement was repealed after QPC agreed to a new agreement which would allow the state to increase its share in both companies to 60 per cent.

In December 1974, the government officially announced its intent to acquire SCQ's and QPC's remaining shares. A government decree passed in 1975 declared government ownership of the remaining shares.

SELECTED REFERENCES

[1] Sorkhabi, Rasoul. *The Qatar Oil Discoveries.* GEO ExPro Magazine, Vol. 7, No. 1 - 2010.

El Mallakh, Ragaei. *Qatar: Development of an Oil Economy.* Croom Helm, London and St Martin's Press, New York 1979

El Mallakh, Ragaei. *Qatar: Energy and Development.* Croom Helm, London and St Martin's Press, New York 1985.

Nafi, Zuhair Ahmed. *Economic and Social Development in Qatar* . Frances Pinter, London and Dover, New Hampshire 1983

Sadik, Muhammed T. and Snavely, William P. *Bahrain, Qatar and the United Arab Emirates.* D.C. Heath, Lexington, Mass. 1972

Graham, Helga. *Arabian Time Machine: Self-Portrait of an Oil State.* Heinemann, London 1978.

Al-Othman, Nasser. *With Their Bare Hands. The Story of the Oil Industry in Qatar.* Longman, London 1984.

Chapter 3

Monetary History of Qatar: Its Evolution within the Middle East and the Gulf States [1]

The history of money in Qatar and the Arabian Peninsula followed that found in other parts of the world. After experimenting with a variety of objects as a medium of exchange, metallic coins came into use as money. Owing to the early trade with East Africa, India and other Asian countries non-metallic money circulated in the region before fully-fledged coins were introduced.

The most widely circulated of these coins were the Maria Theresa thaler and the Indian rupee. The former was first minted in Austria in 1780. The two coins were introduced into the region through international trade. The Indian silver rupee was the dominant currency circulating in Qatar prior to the introduction of paper money. The Maria Theresa thaler was widely used as a medium of exchange along the southern coast of the Arabian Peninsula.

The traditional disadvantages inherent in a metallic currency system caused its abandonment and led to the extensive use of paper money throughout the Arabian Peninsula. This was with the exception of Saudi Arabia which continued to use only coins into the second half of the 20th century.

In Qatar, the difficulty in transporting large amounts of coins and their limited use for larger transactions made them an unstable monetary unit and resulted in the emergence of the Indian rupee as the principal currency.

This continued until May 1959 when the Indian government, in an attempt to stop a black market occurring in the currency, issued a new rupee to be used in the Gulf states. The value of the Gulf rupee, as it was named, was at par with the Indian rupee (0.186621 grammes of fine gold).

Further currency developments in the Gulf consisted of the issue of national currencies, the establishment of central monetary authorities and currency boards.

Qatar was among those countries which did not jump from a Gulf rupee standard directly to a Qatar national currency system. Instead, a currency authority was established for Qatar and Dubai. These and future financial developments took place against the background of rapid political and economic change.

Qatar achieved full independence in 1971 together with other members of the so-called Trucial states.

There was a natural desire among these new nations to have their own monetary systems.

The discovery of oil in Qatar in the 1930s gradually but consistently increased the rate of monetisation of the Qatari economy. See Chapter 2 for more discussion of this.

Monetary History of Qatar

Indian rupees circulated in Qatar until April 28, 1959 when the Gulf rupee, issued by the Reserve Bank of India, was created for use in the Persian Gulf. In June 1966, the Saudi Riyal replaced the Gulf rupee as the medium of exchange in Qatar.

The Qatar and Dubai Currency Board introduced the Qatar-Dubai riyal at par with the Saudi riyal in September 1966. The Qatar-Dubai riyal remained the medium of exchange whilst Qatar was part of the Federation of Arab Emirates, a planned but never realised amalgamation of Bahrain and Qatar and the states of what became the United Arab Emirates, that was agreed in February 1968.

After the state of Qatar was established, Qatar issued its own currency, the Qatari riyal. The Qatar Monetary Agency issued banknotes from 1966 until 1973. The Qatar Central Bank began issuing banknotes in 1973.

Sterling Area and the Middle East [2 3 4]

The development of the banking and financial system in Qatar, as in many other states in the region, was greatly affected by the political and economic factors prevalent during Qatar's recent past.

Politically, Qatar was under British influence until the early 1970s, as a result of which it had economically all the features of the countries linked to the sterling area.

The sterling area system originated in the first half of the nineteenth century. It can be seen as a process of bringing some order into the heterogeneous coinage systems and rudimentary banking arrangements which then prevailed in most of the British colonies and certainly in the Middle East.

The role played by the sterling area in the evolution of financial arrangements in the Middle East region, including Qatar, is discussed below.

The greater degree of political independence which the Arab countries of the Middle East secured, following the end of the Second World War, left unsolved the problem of how to gain more economic independence.

Of all the economic problems facing the Middle East countries, at the time, the problem of handling their foreign currency reserves was one of the most pressing.

The sterling area arrangement had four key characteristics:

i. Local issue currencies and banknotes were statutorily regulated as local versions of the pound sterling and were all printed or stamped with local symbols.

ii. All the participants looked to the City of London as their financial centre for the employment of surplus funds. Due to a shortage of local investment opportunities funds could not be invested with the necessary liquidity, in the colonial countries themselves.

iii. As trade increased, all members of the sterling area looked to sterling as the currency for their external transactions.

iv. All members looked to the City of London and the United Kingdom for the raising of new capital, predominantly for private enterprise but largely also for governmental, provincial or municipal issues.

The main feature of the sterling area was that members were prepared to accept sterling freely and to settle any deficits with one another in this currency. The members, other than Britain, held only limited reserves of gold and convertible currencies (other than sterling) and pooled their earnings of those currencies, accepting sterling in return and enjoying free access to the central reserves of the area whenever they had payments to make across the exchanges.

These arrangements grew out of trading and banking relationships in the nineteenth century. It was in fact during the Second World War that the term sterling area was for the first time formally defined.

The area assumed a more systematic arrangement when, after 1939, it began to operate as a single monetary area within which, with few exceptions, freedom of payments was preserved, while at the same time exchange controls were applied by the various members in their relations with outside countries.

The area at the time embraced some thirty currencies, including those of six countries (Burma, Iceland, Ireland, Iraq, Jordan and Libya) which were outside the British Commonwealth, the various currencies of the independent member countries (Australia, New Zealand, India, Pakistan, Ceylon and South Africa), with their fully-fledged central banks, that of Southern Rhodesia, which had a currency board, and also the currencies of some twenty colonies and other dependent territories, most of which had currency boards rather than central banks as their monetary authorities.

In 1947 Egypt, Iraq, Transjordan and Palestine were members of the sterling area. This membership placed serious constraints on the freedom of action of the respective governments. The practice of maintaining a one-to-one relationship between the volume of domestic money in circulation and foreign currency reserves prevented the governments concerned from exercising any real monetary autonomy.

There was the additional difficulty of obtaining hard currencies in exchange for sterling. This was a particular problem after the suspension of convertibility following the beginning of the Second World War in 1939.

Before illustrating how the sterling area and the Middle East currencies evolved the place of the sterling area, and where Bahrain fitted, needs to be placed in its historical perspective.

The Origins of the Sterling Area

The origins of the sterling area lie in Britain's central position in the global economy before the First World War. For close to a century, the pound sterling functioned as by far the most important international currency, and the City of London as by far the world's most important financial centre.

The largest proportion of global trade was financed, invoiced and settled in sterling; the largest proportion of foreign assets were denominated in sterling; and the largest proportion of official reserves, apart from gold, were held in sterling.

Different economies, however, were attached to the pound sterling with varying degrees of firmness. Sterling was a core of concentric circles, with the closest circles occupied by British colonies and other dependent territories (protectorates, mandates, etc.), by the self-governing commonwealth dominions (except Canada, whose main economic connections had always been with the United States), and by other countries with close commercial and financial ties to Britain (e.g. Ireland, the Scandinavian and Baltic nations, parts of the Balkans, Portugal, Iran and Thailand). For those in the closest circles, it made obvious sense to preserve existing links to the pound after Britain's decision to suspend convertibility in September 1931. Collectively, the economics that did so became known as the sterling bloc.

In the 1930s, members of the bloc were effectively identified by two main characteristics. Firstly, they maintained their currencies in a fixed relationship with sterling even after suspension of gold convertibility, thus continuing their need to use the pound as an exchange-rate peg, and secondly, they also held their external reserves largely if not wholly in the form of sterling balances in London, thus continuing to use the pound as their principal reserve medium of exchange.

For sovereign governments participation was a purely voluntary decision. Until the Second World War the bloc functioned on an informal and strictly non-political basis, with neither a written constitution nor central administration. It was simply an informal grouping of economies with mutually close commercial and monetary connections.

The rationale, essentially, was to minimize the effects of the outside pressure of adverse economic forces. In an era of unprecedented exchange instability and proliferating national restrictions, the bloc's system of ad hoc financial arrangements offered members the continuing benefits of substantial currency stability and freedom of capital movements.

With the outbreak of hostilities in 1939 the group was formalised for the first time to become a clearly circumscribed and statutory entity. As Britain sought to protect its scarce gold and dollar reserves, a comprehensive system of exchange controls was regarded as being imperative. But since preservation of the international monetary functions of sterling was also considered important London chose to erect its controls around the whole of the group of sterling-associated countries rather than around Britain alone, including Qatar.

Until the outbreak of World War Two in 1939, the currencies of the sterling area were freely convertible into US dollars and other currencies, and no attempt was made to control trade through exchange regulations. In September 1939, however, rigid exchange controls were introduced throughout the sterling area with the exception of Iraq, which did not follow suit until November 1941.

The Sterling Area and the Middle East

As can be seen from Table 3.1 and Figure 3.1 there was a gradual build up in overseas sterling area holdings (UK liabilities) and also those of the Middle East countries, including Qatar, during the period 1945 to 1962.

Table 3.1 Overseas sterling holdings and overseas sterling area countries 1945 –1962

	UK liabilities	
End of period	Total	Middle East
1945	2,348	-
1946	2,335	1
1947	2,239	1
1948	2,165	8
1949	2,176	8
1950	2,598	19
1951	2,745	19
1952	2,569	36
1953	2,800	61
1954	2,920	101
1955	2,874	170
1956	2,842	212
1957	2,727	248
1958	2,642	312
1959	2,852	340
1960	2,685	370
1961	2,812	388
1962	2,866	416

Source: Sterling balances: monthly report on external finance, Bank of England Archives EID/98-106

Table 3.2 and Figure 3.1 highlight that during the period 1949-1958 there was a substantial increase in the sterling holdings of Iraq, Jordan and Libya. The sterling holding of the Arabian Gulf countries, including Qatar, grew from no holdings at all in 1949 to £260 million by 1958.

Table 3.2 Middle Eastern share of Overseas Sterling Area holders 1949–1958 £m

	Iraq	Jordan	Arabian Gulf	Libya
1949	49	0	0	0
1950	52	15	0	0
1951	51	14	3	1
1952	60	14	15	6
1953	83	15	38	7
1954	103	19	70	11
1955	116	22	136	11
1956	127	27	169	15
1957	96	29	203	15
1958	101	33	260	18

Source: Sterling balances: monthly report on external finance, Bank of England Archives EID/98-106

Figure 3.1 Middle East Sterling Area 1949-1958

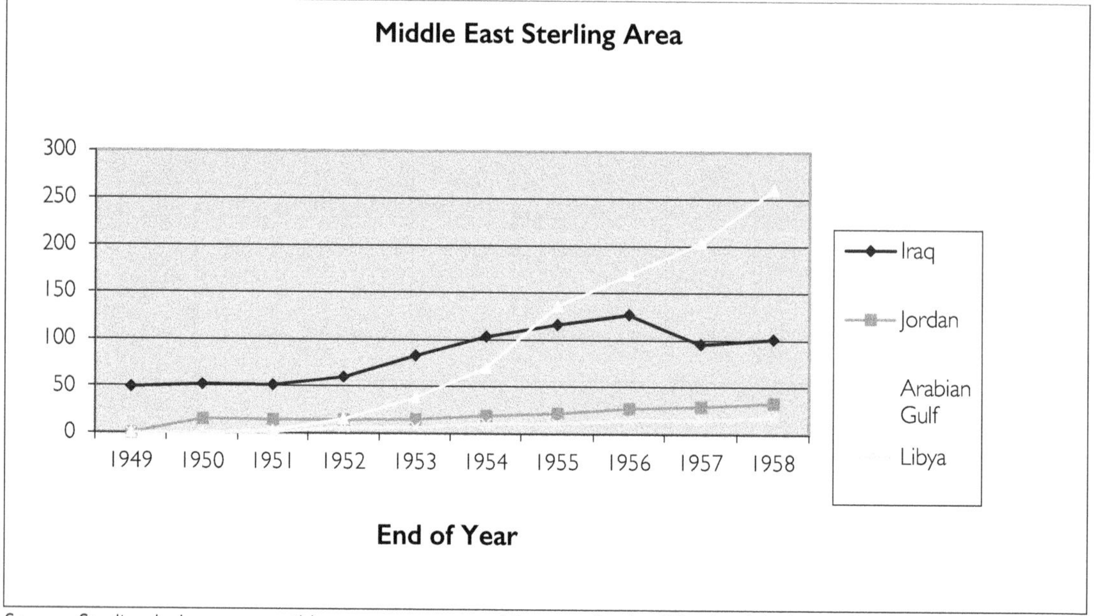

Source: Sterling balances: monthly report on external finance, Bank of England Archives EID/98-106

The Breakup of the Sterling Area

At the end of the Second World War the sterling area stood as the largest and most coherent currency bloc in the world, providing full freedom or payments for all its members. Within the group, overseas participants enjoyed not only the benefits of stable exchange rates but also uninterrupted access to the financial resources of the City of London.

The British government, meanwhile, was able to use the pooled reserves of the entire area's membership to back sterling at a time of a severe dollar shortage. Decline soon set in, however, as Britain's once central position in global affairs began to shrink at an accelerating rate. With the onset of decolonisation came a further contraction of the group, as a number of former dependencies either opted to leave or were excluded, including Israel (after partition of Mandatory Palestine), Egypt, Iraq, and Burma.

The end of the sterling area was not long in coming. In 1972, as the pound was floated, Britain's exchange-control regulations were redefined to encompass no more than the United Kingdom, Ireland, the Isle of Man, the Channel Islands and Gibraltar – in effect, excluding all other economies from the statutory area. On 24 October 1979, all foreign exchange controls on sterling were abolished, and the sterling area as a legal entity was formally dissolved.

Table 3.3 and Figure 3.2 highlights the fall in the share of Middle East overseas sterling holdings, including those of Qatar, during the period 1945-1962. The Middle East share fell from £630 million in 1945 to £133 million by 1962.

Table 3.3 Overseas sterling area holdings 1945- 1962

	UK Liabilities £m	
	Total	**Middle East**
1945	1,254	630
1946	1,329	619
1947	1,343	552
1948	1,087	510
1949	1,083	473
1950	1,067	421
1951	1,085	371
1952	838	308
1953	885	325
1954	994	352
1955	943	323
1956	837	310
1957	311	252
1958	970	257
1959	946	202
1960	1,577	185
1961	1,120	128
1962	1,064	133

Source: Sterling balances: monthly report on external finance, Bank of England Archives EID/98-106

Figure 3.2 UK Liabilities 1945-1963

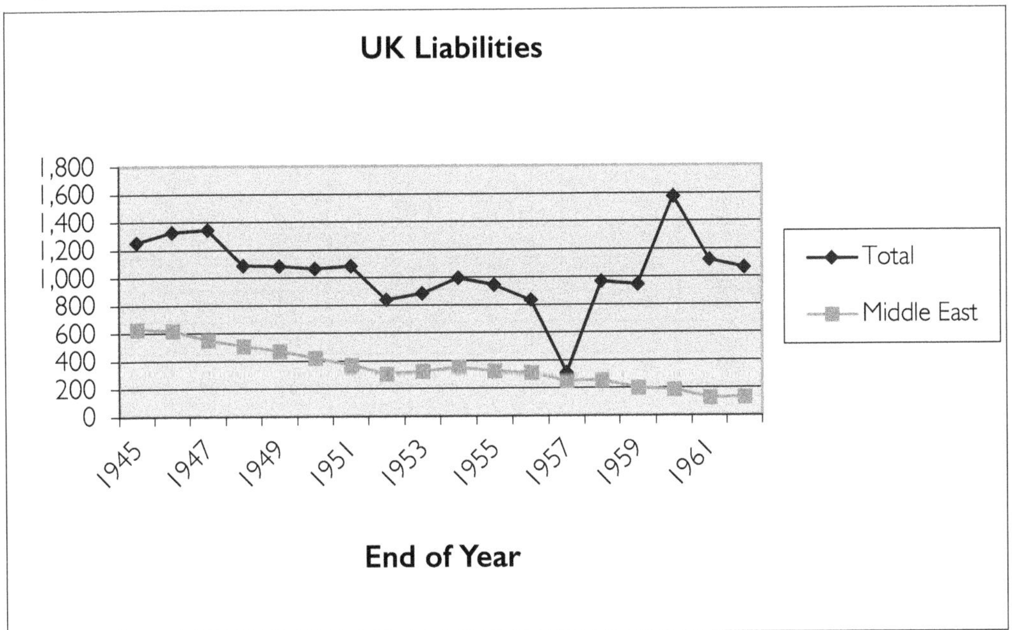

Source: Sterling balances: monthly report on external finance, Bank of England Archives EID/98-106

Table 3.4 highlights the total individual overseas sterling holdings and Middle Eastern share between 1949 and 1958. It can be seen that the Arabian Gulf holdings grew substantially from zero in 1949 to £260 million by 1958.

Table 3.4 Total overseas sterling holdings and Middle Eastern share 1949–1958

	India	Iraq	Jordan	Persian Gulf	Libya	East Africa	Colonies total
IV 1949	822	49	0	0	0	108	673
I 1950	830	49	5	0	0	114	693
II	803	50	5	0	0	125	727
III	794	50	15	0	0	131	860
IV	804	52	15	0	0	139	905
I 1951	823	53	15	0	0	148	979
II	796	52	15	0	0	153	1071
III	771	47	15	0	0	159	1141
IV	730	51	14	3	1	164	1084
I 1952	679	51	13	15	1	172	1107
II	663	48	13	18	6	193	1148
III	682	55	14	16	6	204	1192
IV	694	60	14	15	6	209	1202
I 1953	693	65	13	16	5	214	1245
II	681	74	14	52	6	215	1286
III	675	75	15	45	6	217	1307
IV	697	83	15	38	7	220	1302
I 1954	708	87	15	37	9	222	1352
II	696	91	16	52	10	227	1351
III	687	94	17	58	10	225	1384
IV	691	103	19	70	11	217	1394
I 1955	685	103	20	64	10	212	1419
II	677	113	21	93	10	207	1458
III	679	117	22	106	11	203	1446
IV	687	116	22	136	11	197	1447
I 1956	680	120	24	143	13	195	1473
II	528	124	24	157	13	197	1469
III	475	129	25	164	14	192	1477
IV	412	127	27	169	15	192	1454
I 1957	412	124	26	157	16	194	1483
II	360	108	29	185	16	193	1477
III	290	103	30	189	15	186	1450
IV	254	96	29	203	15	184	1438
I 1958	221	91	31	206	16	181	1454
II	183	90	31	245	15	175	1455
III	155	90	33	256	17	173	1444
IV	156	101	33	260	18	170	1448

Source: Sterling balances: monthly report on external finance. Bank of England Archives EID/98-106

Table 3.5 also highlights total overseas sterling holdings and the Middle Eastern share 1945-60 with the data being more aggregated. These statistics include Egypt and Iraq even though they were in the sterling area only until July 1947 and June 1959 respectively. Middle East overseas sterling holdings grew substantially during this period. It should be noted that the Middle East non-sterling overseas holders fell substantially during this period.

Table 3.5 Total Overseas Sterling holdings and Middle Eastern share 1945-1960 Gross (and net)

Overseas members of the sterling area (£ million)			Non-Sterling Area countries	
Year	**Total**	**Middle East[1]**	**Total**	**Middle East[2]**
Dec. 1945	2348 (2327)	- (-1)	1254 (1240)	630 (628)
March 1950	2321 (2249)	8 (7)	1056 (928)	477 (467)
March 1955	2920 (2801)	96 (95)	1050 (816)	354 (340)
March 1960	2828 (2653)	322 (320)	974 (692)	164 (135)

Notes:
1. Arabian Gulf, Jordan and Libya
2. Egypt, Iran, Iraq, Israel, Lebanon, Saudi Arabia, Sudan and the Yemen
Source: *Bank of England Statistical Abstract 1970, pp. 126-7.*

The British colonies had their currencies given to them by London and were linked to sterling whether they liked it or not. The parities of the colonial currencies were defined in terms of the pound sterling. Their reserves did not consist partly, or mainly, but completely of sterling. Hence, their fate depended altogether on that of the pound sterling.

The Currency Board Period

With the growing oil wealth came the need for a Qatari national currency. Following the formula which Britain had used widely in its overseas territories and colonies, the 'colonial exchange system' was introduced in most of the Arabian Peninsula countries which were under the protection of Britain. [5 6 7]

In 1966 a currency agreement was signed between Qatar and Dubai to establish the Qatar-Dubai Currency Authority (QDCA). Like all currency boards, its functions were limited to the issue and redemption of currency which was backed, at least 100 per cent, by the sterling reserves of the two countries. This made the currency issued by the QDCA a 'sterling surrogate'.

The currency authority restricted its operations to commercial banks and the government. It is doubtful if the QDCA was able to perform the function of banker to the government and commercial banks.

The Qatar-Dubai Currency Authority (QDCA) was established by the signing of a currency agreement between Qatar and Dubai on 21 March 1966. However, the issuing of the Qatar-Dubai riyal was not immediate.

The devaluation of the Gulf rupee, to which the riyal was tied in June 1966 caused the introduction of the new currency to be postponed until 18 September 1966. In the six-month interim, the QDCA borrowed 100 million Saudi Arabian riyals for circulation in the two member countries, in place of the Gulf rupee. See Appendix 5.1 for more details of the QDCA Law

The issue of the Qatar-Dubai riyal valued at 0.186621 grammes of fine gold (i.e., at par with the pre-devaluation Gulf rupee) was important not only for Qatar and Dubai but also for the Trucial states – Bahrain, Oman and the sheikhdoms comprising the United

Arab Emirates with the exception of Abu Dhabi – where the Qatar-Dubai riyal became the sole legal tender currency for some time.

The Qatar Monetary Agency Era

The currency board system became, over time , too restrictive. In Qatar the oil boom in the 1970s made the establishment of a separate central monetary authority imperative. On 19 May 1973, the Qatar Monetary Agency (QMA) was established by royal decree. See Appendix 5.5 for details of the QMA Law.

That law gave the QMA the traditional powers of a fully fledged central bank. These powers included the issue and redemption of currency, safeguarding the internal and external value of the Qatar riyal, promotion of credit and exchange conditions conducive to economic growth and monetary stability and the monitoring of the banks and the financial system. It should be noted that these functions of the QMA did not include explicitly serving as the banker to the government.

The functions of safeguarding the external and internal value of the riyal, ensuring its convertibility and promoting credit and exchange conditions favourable to development could be performed efficiently only if commercial bank credit operations could be controlled and if the QMA held government credit instruments.

The broad manner in which the functions of the QMA were specified in the 1973 law was an indication of the flexibility given to the monetary authority in its attempts to exert control over the Qatar monetary system.

The close relationship with, and almost complete control by the government of Qatar, constituted a break with the older version of central banking legislation.

The QMA was completely owned by the government of Qatar and the seven members of the Board of Directors. These were appointed by the emir upon the recommendation of the Minister of Finance.

Banking and Monetary Developments in Qatar up to the Creation of the Qatar Monetary Agency

The development of the banking and financial system in Qatar, as in many other states in the region, was greatly affected by the political and economic factors prevalent during Qatar's recent past.

Politically, Qatar was under British influence until the early 1970s as a result of which it had economically all the features of the countries linked to the Sterling Area.

Gulf Currency Boards and the Issue of Currency

In most countries of the Arabian Peninsula the functioning of currency boards was based on formulae the British had used for several of their overseas territories and colonies giving rise to what was referred to as the 'colonial sterling exchange standard' or more commonly as the 'colonial currency system'.

As Edo [5] demonstrates the currency board's function was to issue and redeem a currency that was in effect a sterling surrogate. Issues and redemptions of the currency were made locally on demand against the deposit or payment of sterling in London at a fixed sterling rate, with the board charging a small commission on each transaction. The board's transactions were for amounts exceeding a stated minimum, in practice restricting its operations to the commercial banks and government treasury. The general public obtained the currency it needed from the commercial banks.

Currency board principles and their applications to Qatar are discussed in more detail in Chapters 4 and 5.

The currency board was required to maintain a 100 per cent cover for the currency in foreign assets. In fact this cover was mainly held in government securities. There was a cover limit (usually 110 per cent of liabilities) beyond which any net income would be transferred to the government treasury.

Currency boards originated in the British colonies where they were established primarily with a view to creating stable monetary conditions, whilst retaining seigniorage in the local area.

The sole function of the colonial currency boards was to issue banknotes and coins against sterling deposits in London, and vice versa. This was achieved by exchanging local currency for sterling. Most currency boards were based in the local area but some had their headquarters in London.

The currency board countries were required to observe a number of rules:

1. The exchange rate against the anchor currency had to be fixed.
2. A currency board could not influence interest rates in the money market. The colonial currency boards thereby did not include monetary-policy instruments such as official interest rates.

However, in most cases this did not present any major problems. Due to the economic structure in many colonies the banks often had restricted opportunities for investment in the local economies and the volume of bank deposits was limited to banknotes and coins in circulation. Many banks were direct branches of British banks and the colonial banks generally held a major part of their assets in London. The banks functioned to a great extent as exchange bureaux. The individual currency boards had no discretionary powers and fluctuations in the foreign exchange reserves had a direct impact on domestic liquidity, which consisted primarily of banknotes and coins.

For this reason, the assets of a currency board had to be held in safe, readily negotiable government securities within the British Empire rather than in domestic financial assets, even when the latter existed.

The operations of the currency board were automatic and passive in character. The board was in effect a currency changer. As a rule, it had no regulatory powers over the commercial banks, no powers to affect credit and no role in determination of official monetary policy.

This limited concept was the basis of the currency boards established in the years 1960-70 by Qatar and Dubai, Bhrain, Kuwait, the Yemen Arab Republic, the South Arabian Federation and Oman. All these boards issued currencies which replaced the foreign coins and notes previously circulating in the area.

The issuance of the rial Saidi by the Oman Currency Board on 9 May 1970 was of historic importance as it ended the long period during which the Maria Theresa thaler and the Gulf rupee were used as legal tender in the peninsula.

Qatar and Dubai signed a currency agreement on 21 March 1966. This agreement set up a currency authority which was to issue a new currency, the Qatar-Dubai riyal. The June 1966 devaluation of the rupee occurred before this new currency could be introduced.

On 18 September 1966 the Qatar-Dubai riyal was introduced and became the sole legal tender for the two countries concerned as well as the principal currency in the other Trucial states, with the exception of Abu Dhabi.

Box 3.1 illustrates the underlying principles.

Box 3.1 Characteristics of the Qatar-Dubai Currency Board

CURRENCY BOARD Issues local currency.	**LOCAL BANK** Receives local currency.	**LOCAL BANK** Debits its London branch sterling account in favour of the Qatar- Dubai currency board.	**CURRENCY BOARD** Sterling account credited. Receives sterling. Invests sterling in sterling assets (UK government securities).
CURRENCY BOARD Redeems local currency.	**LOCAL BANK** Pays in local currency.	**LOCAL BANK** Credits its London Sterling branch account against the Qatar-Dubai currency board.	**CURRENCY BOARD** Sterling account debited. Pays out sterling Forced to redeem sterling assets (UK government securities).

History of Currencies in Qatar Bahrain and the United Arab Emirates

The Trucial States (Abu Dhabi, Ajman, Dubai, Fujairah, Sharjah, and Umm Al Quwain) were a British protectorate from March 1892 until 2 December 1971 when the six emirates became the United Arab Emirates, Joined by Ras Al Khaimah in February 1972..

Indian rupees circulated in Bahrain until 28 April 1959, when the Gulf rupee, issued by the Reserve Bank of India, was created for use in the Persian Gulf. The Trucial states began using the Bahraini dinar in June 1966 with 1 Bahrain dinar equal to 10 Gulf rupees.

In September 1966, all the Trucial states with the exception of Abu Dhabi,, adopted the Qatar-Dubai riyal (QDR) as their medium of exchange. Abu Dhabi continued to use the Bahraini dinar until 2 December 1971 when the United Arab Emirates dirham, divisible into 1000 fils replaced the Qatar-Dubai riyal at par.

Bahraini dinar were interchangeable with UAE dirhams from 1 January 1976 until 5 May 1979 at the rate of 1 dinar equal to 10 dirhams, and Qatar riyals were interchangeable with UAE dirhams at par from 1 September 1976 until 5 May 1979.

The Qatar Bahrain Abu Dhabi Monetary System

Chapter 5 discusses the monetary system in Qatar, Bahrain and Abu Dhabi with regard to the currency in circulation and related monetary implications in more detail than here.

Neither in the past nor in the present has Abu Dhabi had a currency of its own. In the past, the Gold Sterling guinea, the silver Maria Theresa thaler and the Indian rupee were in circulation. Turkish currency was used during the time of the Ottoman Empire, but only to a limited extent. The circulation of these currencies, especially the Indian rupee, was attributed to the commercial relations which linked Abu Dhabi to India including trade and exchange since bygone times.

In 1958, the Indian government considered the issuance of the rupee currency for circulation in the Gulf through the Reserve Bank of India. This was to limit smuggling of currency from India, especially gold.

Abu Dhabi issued a red coloured Gulf rupee in circulation, as of 1958, to distinguish it from the Indian blue coloured rupee.

On 6 June 1966, the Indian government devalued the rupee by 35 per cent and the banks in Abu Dhabi closed until they could discern whether the devaluation applied to the Indian rupee in circulation in the Gulf. The answer came ten days later stating that the devaluation applied to the rupee circulating in the Gulf, thus causing material harm to Abu Dhabi, as well as to the other Persian Gulf emirates in which the Indian rupee was also in circulation.

In the wake of that the Abu Dhabi government considered dispensing with the Indian rupee. It had two alternatives; either to issue its own currency or resort to one of the currencies in circulation in the area. It preferred to adopt the circulation of the Bahraini dinar as a temporary solution, in July 1966.

SELECTED REFERENCES

[1]Appendices 1 to 4 provide detailed breakdowns of the Middle East and Gulf currency arrangements for the relevant periods for this text.

[2] Clauson, G.L.M. *The British Colonial Currency System.* Economic Journal, Vol. 54, p1-25. 1944

[3]Greaves, I. *The Colonial Sterling Balances. Essays in International Finance No. 20, International Finance Section, Princeton University.* Princeton University Press 1954

[4]Hazelwood, Arthur. *The Economics of Colonial Monetary Arrangements.* Sir Arthur Lewis Institute of Social and Economic Studies, The University of the West Indies, Vo.3 (Nos. 3-4), p291-315 1954

[5]Edo, Michael E. *Currency Arrangements and Banking Legislation in the Arabian Peninsula.* International Monetary Fund, Middle Eastern Department. Washington, DC 1974

[6]Shannon, H.A. *The Modern Colonial Sterling Exchange Standard.* IMF Staff Papers, Vol. 2, p318-62 1952

[7]Thornton, A.P. *Imperialism in the Twentieth Century.* Minneapolis: University of Minnesota Press 1977

Colonial Office. *Memorandum on the Sterling Assets of the British Colonies. Colonial No. 298.* HMSO (British colonies), London 1953

Caine, Sir Sydney. *Monetary Systems of the Colonies.* The Banker. F.J.Parsons, London 1950.

Sayers, Richard S. ed. *Banking in the British Commonwealth.* Oxford University Press, Oxford 1952.

The Sterling Area. Bank for International Settlements, Basel 1953.

Quarterly Bulletin. Bank of England, March1962.

Conan, A. R. *The Sterling Area.* Macmillan, London 1952

Harrod, R. F. *The Pound Sterling. Essays in International Finance No. 13, International Finance Section, Princeton University.* Princeton University Press, 1952

Chapter 4

Currency Boards: Predecessors of Central Banks

What is an Orthodox Currency Board?[1]

An orthodox currency board is an institution that issues notes and coins convertible on demand at a fixed exchange rate into a foreign currency or other external reserve asset.

An orthodox currency board does not accept deposits. It holds low-risk, interest bearing bonds and other assets denominated in the so-called anchor currency. It generates profits from the difference between the interest rate earned on its reserve assets and the expenses of maintaining its liabilities, these being the notes and coins in circulation.

Unorthodox currency boards do not fulfil all these criteria.

The features of the modern orthodox currency board did not become well established until 1913, 64 years after the first currency board was established. Currency boards established before 1913 differed from later orthodox currency boards, most notably in the type of external assets they held.

Currency Board Principles

The forerunners of central banks in the Gulf/Middle East were currency boards. In this chapter we examine the principles underlying currency boards before going on to examine the Qatar Currency Board in more detail in Chapter 5.

At that stage empirical tests as to whether the board conformed to the theory are tested by the Author.

Currency boards can usefully be classified at opposite ends of the spectrum as being either orthodox or unorthodox with variants in between.

Appendix 4.1 sets out the currency board principles as set out by a practitioner.

Are Currency Boards Central Banks?

A currency board is *not* a central bank.

The essential difference between them is that a currency board maintains a fixed proportion of reserves as foreign assets, whereas a central bank does not. The power to vary the ratio of external assets to domestic liabilities enables a central bank to engage in discretionary sterilisation of the reserves of commercial banks.

In contrast a currency board sacrifices any flexibility in its ability to apply discretionary monetary policy.

The following are the characteristics of orthodox currency boards:

1. Fixed exchange rate against the anchor currency
2. Unrestricted convertibility into the anchor currency
3. Net foreign reserves greater than monetary liabilities
4 No discretionary monetary policy and severely constrained fiscal policy

5 No sterilisation of the monetary effects of foreign exchange flows
6. Interest rates determined by those of the anchor currency
7. Seigniorage associated with the issue of domestic coins and notes is earned by the board
8. Encouragement of freedom of entry for foreign banks

1 Fixed exchange rate against the anchor currency

The external "reserve" asset is also often referred to as the anchor currency.

The currency board maintains a fixed exchange rate by being willing to buy or sell domestic currency (currency in circulation) for foreign currency, on demand, at the official exchange rate.

A currency board fully backs its domestic monetary base with foreign exchange and hence cannot run out of reserves in the extreme case of all domestic money holders demanding foreign exchange.

The whole of the domestic money supply is covered by foreign assets.

The effect is that foreign assets become the de facto anchor currency.

2 Unrestricted Convertibility into the Anchor Currency

The currency board system is a system of fixed exchange rates. A currency board exchanges its notes and coins for an external reserve asset and vice versa at a fixed rate (See Box 4.1).

Most currency boards have used securities denominated in a single foreign currency as their reserve asset, so it is normal to refer to the reserve asset as the reserve currency, or alternatively as the anchor currency.

A currency board may charge a small fee to cover the costs of exchange transactions, but it need not, given that its interest earnings should far exceed its expenses.

The currency board system allows complete convertibility of currency board notes and coins into the reserve currency.

Because bank deposits are convertible into currency board notes and coins at a fixed rate (e.g. £1 of bank deposits = £1 of local notes and coins), bank deposits are also convertible into the reserve currency. However, the currency board bears no responsibility for converting bank deposits into currency board notes and coins. Banks must keep on hand adequate reserves of currency board notes and coins to satisfy customer demand to liquidate deposits.

Unlike a central bank, a currency board does not act as a lender of last resort to the banking system.

The currency board is typically not the only holder of reserve currency in a currency board system. Banks can, and will, also hold reserve currency. Persons who wish to convert deposits of domestic currency into foreign currency can do so directly, by exchanging domestic currency deposits for foreign currency with their bank, or indirectly, by cashing in the deposits for currency board notes and exchanging the notes for foreign currency at the currency board.

Another characteristic of a currency board system, in this context, is that there are no exchange controls.

Capital inflows and outflows are unrestricted. A currency board stands ready to convert all its own currency into reserve currency on demand at the fixed exchange rate. It also stands ready to accept unlimited amounts of reserve currency for conversion into its domestic currency. See Box 4.1.

Box 4.1 Currency Board Intervention Principles

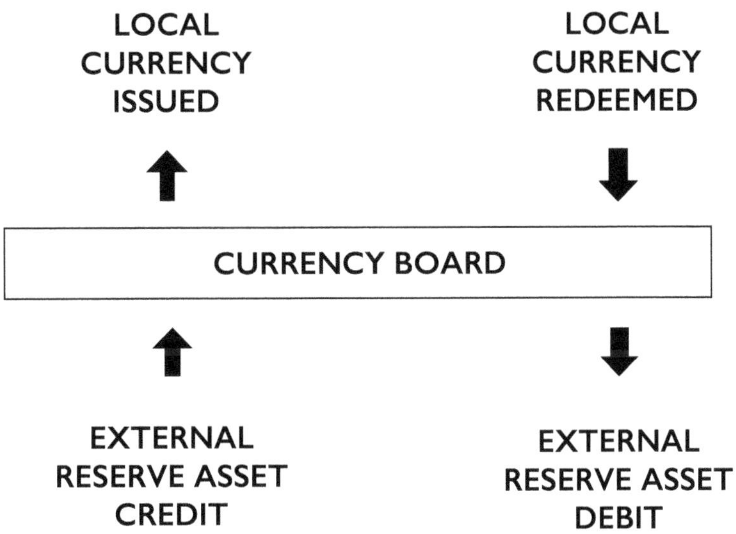

1. Currency Board issues (redeems) local currency to local banks.
2. Local bank debits (credits) its external reserve assets or those of the currency board.
3. Currency board buys (sells) external reserve assets and invests in (divests from) external reserve assets (government securities) and earns (loses) future income.
4. Net foreign reserves are greater than monetary liabilities.

To qualify as acceptable foreign exchange reserves an orthodox currency board must hold high-quality, interest-bearing securities denominated in the reserve asset.

Its reserve ratio is fixed at 100 per cent or slightly more of its notes and coins in circulation. The effect is that a currency board holds external assets equal to at least 100 per cent of the board's notes and coins in circulation. The assets are sometimes actual foreign currency but, far more commonly, securities issued abroad and denominated in the reserve currency.

External assets of 100 per cent ensure that even if all holders of notes and coins want to convert into the reserve currency, the currency board will be able to do so.

An orthodox currency board will hold a portion of its reserves in extremely liquid form, such as bank deposits in the reserve currency country and top-grade short-term securities. If conditions permit, it may also hold some reserves in less liquid but higher-yielding forms, such as long-term securities.

In addition to their 100 per cent reserve against notes and coins in circulation, past currency boards have usually accumulated, from profits, an additional reserve of 5 to 10 per cent to provide for a margin of protection should their liquid investments lose value.

Although an orthodox currency board must cover its domestic currency liabilities with external reserve assets it cannot cover them by too large a margin. If it does so, then the automaticity of changes in foreign currency inflows on the domestic monetary base will break down. If a currency board uses its excess reserves in a discretionary fashion, say by sterilised intervention, it is no longer orthodox.

Some commentators have suggested that some safety margin is acceptable but once the reserve cover goes over 110 per cent then the currency board is no longer orthodox.

See Box 4.2 to illustrate a hypothetical example of a currency board.

Chapter 5 discusses the Qatar Currency Board in detail.

Appendix 5.2 highlights the Qatar Currency Board balance sheet.

Box 4.2 A hypothetical example of the balance sheet of a currency board

Balance sheet for an orthodox currency board

ASSETS		LIABILITIES	
Foreign Assets	$1500	Deposits held in banks	$500
Domestic Assets	$0	Currency in circulation	$1000
Total Assets	$1500	Total Liabilities	$1500

An orthodox currency board is prohibited from acquiring any domestic assets. It must only hold foreign reserve assets.

3 Monetary and Fiscal Policy

By design, a currency board has *no* discretionary power when it comes to monetary policy. Its monetary policy is completely automatic, consisting only of exchanging its notes and coins for the reserve currency at a fixed rate.

One of the arguments in favour of a currency board is that it can be more insulated from politics than that of a central bank.

A currency board officially removes monetary policy from the hands of politicians. The currency board country implicitly adopts the monetary policy of the anchor currency country.

The authorities cannot increase the money supply without tending to lower the public's perception of the external value of the currency. At that stage the public may choose to convert their domestic currency into the anchor currency.

If the anchor country increases the supply of its currency, the currency board will have to buy more foreign currency and issue more of its domestic currency. As a result, the country adopting the currency board system loses all control of its monetary policy.

An orthodox currency board has no discretion in monetary policy, as mentioned above. It plays a purely passive money changer type role supplying or buying foreign currency for domestic currency on demand. Market forces alone determine the quantity of notes and coins in circulation.

As Schuler points out it was not until the late 1940s and the 1950s that economists inquired into the workings of the money supply in a currency board system. (1) By then, currency boards had existed for a century. The theory of currency boards lagged well behind the practice.

How did the Money Supply change in the Qatar Currency Board system?

Suppose that a British manufacturer has a factory in Qatar (a former currency board country), and the manufacturer pays factory wages in the local currency (Qatari riyals). To do so it deposits sterling notes with a bank in the UK. The bank then deposits the sterling with the Qatar Currency Board.

The currency board gives the bank Qatari riyals for every £1 sterling, because that is the fixed rate at which it exchanges Qatari notes and coins for the reserve currency, sterling. The factory in Qatar then pays the factory wages by withdrawing Qatari riyals from the Qatari branch of the bank.

The outcome of all this is that the Qatari money supply increases by the amount of the wage payments.

The process also works in reverse. Suppose a resident of Qatar wishes to make a cash down payment on a house in the UK. He takes Qatari riyal notes and visits a local bank. The bank exchanges the notes at the Qatar Currency Board for an equivalent number of sterling notes. The resident of Qatar uses the sterling notes to make the down payment on the house.

The outcome is the opposite of the previous example. The Qatari money supply falls by the amount of the down payment on the house.

The examples just given are the simplest cases: exchanges of notes for notes. If a Qatari factory worker wishes to deposit with local banks some of the notes the workers have been paid, the banks reserves increase.

Currency board notes count as reserves for banks in a currency board system just as central bank notes do in a central banking system. The banks increased reserves may then become the basis for a multiple expansion of bank credit of the type familiar from elementary textbooks on money and banking.

On the other hand, if the resident of Qatar makes the down payment on the house in the UK, not by exchanging notes he has kept under his mattress, but by converting a Qatari riyal deposit to a sterling deposit, the Qatari banking system loses reserves and a multiple contraction of bank credit may occur.

Changes of the Qataris public's desired holdings of notes relative to coins could also affect bank reserves, causing multiple expansions or contractions of bank credit, even if no foreign-exchange transactions occur.

3. Fiscal Policy under a Currency Board System

Government budgets in currency board systems have, on average historically, been balanced or slightly in surplus. In theory, a government can run persistent budget deficits under the currency board system if it can keep borrowing to finance deficits. In practice, lenders are unwilling to allow government budget deficits to persist forever and crowding out would take place thereby putting upward pressure on interest rates and attracting capital inflows.

An orthodox currency board system enforces a hard budget constraint on the domestic government.

4. Monetary Policy and Sterilisation

Sterilisation refers to the extent that domestic credit is varied to offset part, or all, of the effects of capital or trade flows on the money supply.

An orthodox currency board, as mentioned earlier, cannot sterilise inflows or outflows and therefore cannot use monetary policy as a tool of economic policy.

This point requires some explanation. In the discussion below NDC refers to net domestic credit and NFA to net foreign assets. NDC and NFA sum to the monetary base and are derived from the currency board balance sheet, as expressed in domestic currency.

The monetary policies adopted by the authorities, when the exchange rate is fixed can be thought of as being on a spectrum, which show they adjust net domestic credit (NDC) in response to changes in the official foreign exchange reserves.

The change in the supply of base money (M0) is equal to the sum of changes in NDC and changes in net foreign assets (NFA):

$$M0 = NDC + NFA$$
$$\Delta M0 = \Delta NDC + \Delta NFA$$

Where $\Delta M0$, ΔNDC and ΔNFA indicate the changes in M0, NDC and NFA.

The change in official foreign exchange reserves is the dominant element in ΔNFA.

Since a balance of payments surplus/deficit in any period is equal to the change in official foreign exchange reserves, it follows that how the currency board adjusts domestic credit in response to a change in official foreign exchange reserves will determine the overall effect on the money supply of balance of payments surpluses or deficits.

At one end of the spectrum is full sterilisation of the monetary effect of balance of payments flows: the authorities try to hold base money constant by expanding domestic credit if the balance of payments is in deficit and by contracting domestic credit, if it is in surplus.

Chapter 5 and 6 provides examples of how these monetary aggregates evolved in the Qatar Currency Board period.

At the other end of the visible spectrum is an orthodox currency board system under which the board leaves domestic credit unchanged, so that a balance of payments deficit/surplus causes the monetary base to fall/rise dollar-for-dollar with official foreign exchange reserves. (See Box 4.3)

A sterilisation coefficient of unity implies complete sterilization of the monetary effects of foreign exchange inflows; a coefficient of zero implies no sterilisation.

Box 4.3 No sterilisation rule as applied in British currency boards: the case of inflows

Exports rise and /or there are capital inflows.

↓

Sector affected receives sterling.

↓

Pays sterling into the currency board.

↓

Currency board provides currency in exchange,

↓

Domestic money supply rises.

Under the textbook currency board system, the board does not attempt to control domestic credit so that a balance of payments surplus (deficit) causes the monetary base to rise (fall) pound for pound with official foreign exchange reserves.

As an orthodox currency board can only hold foreign reserve assets and cannot hold domestic assets (see Box 4.1), the effect of this is that monetary sterilisation becomes impossible. (See Box 4. 4)

As an orthodox currency board cannot legally hold domestic assets it cannot sterilise foreign exchange operations. This means that it cannot sterilise inflows or outflows and therefore cannot use monetary policy as a tool of economic policy.

To test for whether sterilisation was taking place within a currency board one would have to look for large swings in the ratios of foreign reserves to the monetary base. See Box 4.4.

Box 4.4 Sterilisation Principles: Monetary Policy Reaction

Balance of Payments	Domestic credit and base money	No Sterilisation	Sterilisaton
Surplus	Rises	Neutral	Contractionary
Deficit	Falls	Neutral	Expansionary

Appendix 4.2 details the issues with sterilisation coefficient calculations.

6. Interest rates and inflation

An orthodox currency board is committed to supply or redeem its monetary liabilities at a fixed exchange rate, which implies that it must hold foreign reserves at least equal to its total monetary liabilities.

Moreover, these are the only terms under which a currency board can exchange monetary liabilities. In other words, as discussed earlier, in its orthodox variety a currency board cannot extend credit.

Under these conditions interest rates are not under the control of the domestic monetary authorities. Domestic interest rates will track those of the anchor currency.

Given the fixed exchange rate between the currency board currency and the reserve currency, if trade barriers are low, changes in the prices of tradable goods should be close to those occurring in the reserve currency country. However, consumer price indexes need not move in parallel, because they include non-tradable goods, whose prices may diverge in the two countries.

7. Profits and Seigniorage

The currency board makes profits from the difference between the interest rate on the securities that it holds and the expense of maintaining its notes and coins in circulation. It traditionally remits to the home government all profits beyond which it needs to pay expenses and maintain its reserve ratio.

The fixed exchange rate that a currency board maintains with the reserve currency means that the account holder is using a currency that is as sound (or possibly as unsound) as the reserve currency.

8. Seigniorage issues

Seigniorage revenues (income generated from printing money) are lost under a currency board system.

Any revenue from seigniorage and the inflation tax that goes with it go to the country that issues the anchor currency. Unlike securities or most bank deposits, notes and coins do not pay interest; hence they yield seigniorage to the issuer.

Seigniorage can be considered as a stock or as a flow. To understand it as a stock, consider the notes and coins that people hold. The issuer has made a profit equal to the value of the notes and coins, because it has spent that amount into circulation without losing reserves, acquiring goods from others whilst sacrificing nothing itself.

The flow revenue from seigniorage, on the other hand, equals the nominal interest rate. For the sake of clarity, one can safely assume that the expense of putting the notes and coins into circulation is very low.

The currency board system also had the advantage over direct use of a foreign currency in that it satisfies nationalistic sentiment for a locally issued currency.

9. Banking relationships

The currency board is only a part of the monetary system in any country that has banks and other financial institutions.

Chapter 6 details the growth of the Qatar commercial banking system during the currency board period. See Appendix 6.6 .

The currency board is an important part of commercial banking activities given that it determines what the monetary standard should be. This is by way of the legal tender aspects that governments have usually given to currency board notes and the one-to-one convertibility of bank deposits into currency board notes.

One of the key characteristics of currency board systems is to allow freedom of entry by foreign banks. Because most currency board systems have lacked lenders of last resort, there has always been the need to manage or prevent the effects of systemic risk that can take place should bank failures occur.

Stability in the banking system has, in many currency board countries, been achieved by the fact that most prominent banks in currency board systems have been international banks with extensive branch networks, including branches in the reserve currency country to enable them to tap its money markets readily.

It was deemed important by the authorities to attract banks with strong balance sheets.

See Chapter 6 to illustrate how Qatar dealt with this.

Other aspects of the banking business have also generally been lightly regulated in currency board systems.

An orthodox currency board is not a lender of last resort to commercial banks, unlike a central bank. The government may provide lender of last resort facilities through deposit insurance, but most currency board countries did not do so. Instead, banks in currency board systems developed other methods to remain liquid during financial crises.

Chapter 5 examines the detailed workings of the Qatar Currency Board.

SELECTED REFERENCES

[1] For a more complete discussion of currency boards see following doctoral thesis which this section draws upon: Schuler, Kurt. *Currency Boards. Dissertation.* George Mason University, Fairfax, Virginia 1992. Dr Schuler is a strong supporter of currency boards.

Walters, A. *Currency Boards.* Johns Hopkins University Department of Economics, Working Paper No. 281. 1992

Schwartz, Anna J. *Currency boards: their past, present and possible future role.* Carnegie-Rochester Conference Series on Public Policy, Vol. 39. Elsevier, 1993.

Hanke, Steve H. & Schuler, Kurt . *Currency Boards for Developing Countries: A Handbook.* ICS Press, San Francisco 1994

Roubini, Nouriel. *The Case Against Currency Boards: Debunking 10 Myths about the Benefits of Currency Boards.* Stern School of Business, New York University, February 1998

McLeod, Alexander. *The British Currency-Board System – Successes and Shortcomings.* The Banker, v.125, no.589, Mar., p247-52. 1976

Schuler, Kurt. *No More Central Banks: How to Prevent a Currency Crisis.* Journal of Commerce, May 18, 1999.

Enoch, Charles & Gulde, Anne-Marie. *Are Currency Boards a Cure for All Monetary Problems?* IMF Finance & Development. Volume 35, Number 4, December 1998.

Edo, Michael E. *Character of Currencies of Arabian Peninsula Shaped by Recent Origin: Area's Resources.* International Monetary Fund Survey, v.4, no. 1. 6 Jan, p10-12. 1975

Appendix 4.1

C. E. Loombe on Currency Boards

To get an insight into applying Currency Board principles it is instructive to read the guide below, written by Mr C.E.Loombe, who was the Bank of England's principal adviser on the Middle East and worked for several currency boards.

'The purpose of this note is to set out in general terms the simplest form of currency board and it is assumed that the international currency referred to below is sterling.

The establishment of a currency board provides a simple and inexpensive way of managing a country's currency. The functions of a currency board are generally restricted to the preparation, issue and redemption of the currency, to keeping stocks of unissued currency, to the destruction of currency withdrawn from circulation and to the investment of the assets held as cover against the currency in circulation.

The normal procedure is for the currency board to be set up by local legislation under which it is answerable to the Government concerned and by which its notes and coin issues are the sole legal tender of the country.

A new currency must command confidence, both internally and externally, that it will be exchangeable into an accepted international currency such as sterling or dollars at rates of exchange which vary only within prescribed margins.

This confidence, particularly in the early stages, is normally engendered by statutorily requiring the issuing authority to maintain a fixed percentage of reserves in the form of gold or acceptable reserve currencies and by an obligation to issue and redeem its own currency against a reserve currency, such as sterling.

The main points in the operation of a currency board are:

1. . The maintenance of a fixed parity which is prescribed in the currency legislation. Having established a currency board this parity is maintained through an obligation by the board to issue and redeem local currency against sterling at par, subject to a commission which must not exceed a stated amount. In practice the currency board usually deals only with the banks and not with the public.

   Legally the public are not debarred from access to the board but it is preferable that public transactions should be conducted through the medium of banks. For this reason, a minimum amount of local currency which can be bought or sold at any time is usually stipulated by the board.

2. The statutes would stipulate the assets which the board may hold against the currency circulation.
   To begin with it is suggested that the assets should be 100 per cent sterling and apart from necessary cash balances these would be invested in Treasury Bills and short-term and readily marketable Government securities.

The portfolio would have to be arranged in such a way that the currency board was at all times able to provide on demand sufficient sterling to meet any likely redemption of local currency, i.e. maintenance of a liquid position, but at the same time to secure the maximum interest on the securities commensurate with liquidity.

Some countries hold some part of their cover in gold but gold is non-interest bearing and provided the local currency is linked and backed by one of the reserve currencies, e.g. sterling, there is little object in holding gold.

Any increase or decrease in the circulation is automatically adjusted by the receipt or payment of sterling thus maintaining the 100 per cent sterling cover.

3. A currency board once established aims to meet its expenses out of income. This income consists primarily of the interest received on the assets held as cover against the currency in circulation and also – but in a small degree – of commissions charged on issues and redemptions of currency.

The statutes normally stipulate what shall be done about the distribution of any excess of revenue over expenditure. After the provision of adequate reserves, it is the usual practice for the residue to be paid to Government once any loan by Government to meet initial expenses has been repaid – see paragraph 8.

4. The seat of the board should be in the financial centre of the country. It is preferable not to have too large a board and a satisfactory size is, say, a Chairman with four of five members. Members should be persons experienced in business and finance.

5. The staff requirements for a currency board are small, but the Currency Officer must have the necessary technical qualifications to administer the affairs of the board.

6. It is usual to appoint a bank in the country as currency agent. The main duties of the agent bank would be the safe custody of unissued stocks of currency notes and coins (held under joint control with the currency board); the physical side of the issue and redemption of the currency; the withdrawal of soiled notes from circulation and arrangements in conjunction with the currency board for the destruction of notes unfit for issue.

7. Once a decision has been taken to introduce a new currency it is necessary at an early stage to approach security note printers and mints with a view of deciding on the design of coins and notes and then place orders for their manufacture. At this stage a number of points arise such as the name of the new currency; the sub-divisions and the names of such sub-divisions and the exchange value of the basic unit of the new currency.

8. It is difficult to estimate exactly what the initial cost of establishing a new currency would be. Much depends on the number of notes and particularly the amount of coin required. The Government would have to be prepared to make an initial loan to the board to provide it with working capital. The following table should give some indication of what is involved. It shows the amounts of

Government loans received by some currency boards on establishment and details of expenditure taken from the first year's balance sheet.

Date Established	Country	Government Loan (000s)	Total expenses in first reporting period (000s)	of which: Notes (000s)	of which: Coin (000s)	Currency circulating at end of first reporting period (millions)
1949	Jordan	£55	£95	£30	£39	JD 9.4
1953	Libya	£150	£153	£43	£78	£L 3.6
1956	Sudan	£S350	£S558	£S127	£S354	£S 24.3
1961	Kuwait	KD199	KD140	KD134		KD 30.3

9. The operation of redemption of the external rupees would require the co-operation of the Reserve Bank of India, the commercial banks and the Post Office. Supplies of the new currency should be available by the day of the changeover, and for a period of some (stipulated) weeks after that day both currencies would be legal tender. All the banks and the Post Office could be appointed agents to carry out the exchange of currencies.

. The currency exchange should be given the widest publicity, and leaflets giving details of the exchange facilities, including a conversion table, should be prepared for distribution.

REFERENCE

C.E.Loombe, report for Sayyed Mahmoud Ahmed al Alawi, Director of Finance, Bahrain. 13 January 1964. Bank of England, OV 72-9, 104:106.

Appendix 4.2[1]

The role of Sterilised Intervention

Sterilised intervention for the currency boards needs some explaining.

The calculations below are for a monetary authority that maintains a rigid exchange rate, such as 10 pesos = US$1. The calculations abstract from the effects of gains and losses to reserves arising from reductions in the capital value of foreign assets, interest received, and other factors not related to intervention or lack of it in the money market by the monetary authority. Particularly if the period involved is short, such factors should be small compared to whatever sterilisation has occurred.

1. Convert the central bank balance sheet into a simplified balance sheet showing net foreign assets and net domestic assets, on the one hand, and the monetary base and other liabilities, on the other hand.

a. For example, take this hypothetical balance sheet, which is in a format typical of the IMF's *International Financial Statistics:*

Balance sheet, period 1

Assets (million pesos)		*Liabilities (million pesos)*	
Foreign assets	500	Reserve money	600
Claims on central government	250	Of which, currency outside deposit money banks	550
Claims on deposit money banks	90	Foreign liabilities	100
Claims on other banking institutions	60	Central government deposits	50
		Capital accounts	80
		Other items (net)	70
Total	*900*	*Total*	*900*

b. Calculate the numbers in the simplified balance sheet by using the following identities:

Net foreign assets ≡ foreign assets – foreign liabilities.
Net domestic assets ≡ reserve money – net foreign assets.

Usually foreign assets and liabilities are clearly identified on the balance sheets of monetary authorities, meaning that by implication all other assets and liabilities are domestic. However, there may be cases of deception. For instance, counting local government bonds denominated in foreign currency as a 'foreign' asset is inaccurate; so is hiding foreign assets under 'other items.' In such cases, detective work is necessary.

Note that the IMF's term for the monetary base is 'reserve money' and that currency outside deposit money banks is a component of reserve money, therefore it should not be included separately among the liabilities because that would be double counting.

The simplified balance sheet is as follows:

Simplified balance sheet, period 1

Assets (million pesos)		*Liabilities (million pesos)*	
Net foreign assets = 500 – 100	400	Reserve money	600
Net domestic assets = 600 – 400	200		
Total	*600*	*Total*	*600*

Net foreign assets or net domestic assets may be positive or negative, depending on circumstances. For example, a currency board that holds 660 million pesos of net foreign assets and no net domestic assets against 600 million pesos of reserve money will have *negative* net domestic assets of 60 million pesos according to the simplified balance sheet.

Now suppose the simplified balance sheet from the next period—which could be a day, week, month, quarter, or year later—is as follows:

Simplified balance sheet, period 2

Assets (million pesos)		*Liabilities (million pesos)*	
Net foreign assets	300	Reserve money	550
Net domestic assets	250		
Total	*550*	*Total*	*550*

2. Calculate the change in net foreign assets and in reserve money from period to period.

Comparing the two balance sheets (millions of pesos omitted below), do as follows.

a. Take reserve money in period 2 and subtract from it reserve money in period 1 to find the change between periods: 550 – 600 = -50.
b. Take net foreign assets in period 2 and subtract from it net foreign assets in period 1 to find the change between periods: 300 – 400 = -100.
c. Take the change in reserve money and subtract from it the change in net foreign assets: -50 – (-100) = 50.

This last subtraction shows how the actual change in reserve money compares to the change that would have occurred under a 'no sterilisation' case. Without sterilisation, reserve money would have fallen by 100 million pesos, just as net foreign assets did. Instead, reserve money only fell by 50 million pesos. Therefore, reserve money is 50 million pesos higher than it would have been without sterilisation.

3. Calculate what one might call the raw coefficient of sterilisation by this formula: Difference between actual change in reserve money and 'no sterilisation' case/change in net foreign assets.

That is, divide 2(c) by 2(b): 50 / -100 = -0.5.

If the coefficient is zero, no sterilisation occurred; if it is between 0 and -1, the monetary authority partly sterilised a change in reserves; if it is -1, the monetary authority totally sterilised the change; if it is less than -1 (for instance, -4), the monetary authority changed reserve money in the opposite direction from the change in reserves, by more than the change in reserves. If the coefficient is greater than 0, the monetary authority changed reserve money in the same direction as the change in reserves, but by a greater amount.

For example, if the change in foreign reserves *compared to the 'no sterilisation' case* was -30 million pesos and the change in reserve money was -75 million pesos, the coefficient of sterilisation would be:

(-30 – [-75]) / -30 = 1.5

In this case, the amount by which the monetary authority amplified the change in foreign reserves was 1.5 times the change in foreign reserves. The monetary authority changed the monetary base by -30 million pesos * 1.5 = -45 million pesos more than under the 'no sterilisation' case.

You can see from a little playing around with numbers that the coefficient can range from infinitely negative to infinitely positive. A possible term for this amount is 'net intervention'.

4. Finally, for an idea of the scale of sterilisation, you can compare it to total net foreign assets ('normalising' it).

Sterilisation of 50 million out of 100 million pesos and of 5 out of 10 pesos both give the same raw sterilisation coefficient (-50 million / 100 million = -0.5 and -5 / 10 = -0.5), but the first case is 10 million times as big in absolute terms. The scale of sterilisation in the first case is -0.125 of the net foreign assets in period 1, compared with -0.00000125 in the second case.

[1]I am very grateful to Kurt Schuler and Steve Hancke for providing this Appendix. November 26, 2004

Chapter 5

The Qatar-Dubai Currency Board: Was it a success?

The Qatar-Dubai Currency Board Period [1]

With growing oil wealth came the need for a Qatari national currency. Following the formula which Britain had used widely in its overseas territories and colonies, the 'colonial exchange system' was introduced in most of the Arabian Peninsula countries which were under the protection of Britain. See Chapter 3 for more discussion of this.

In 1966 a currency agreement was signed between Qatar and Dubai to establish the Qatar-Dubai Currency Board. Like all currency boards its functions were limited to the issue and redemption of currency; this being backed by at least 100 per cent by the sterling reserves of the two countries. This made the currency issued by the QDCB a 'sterling surrogate'.

As if attempting to take on a characteristic of a central bank (in addition to those of currency issue and redemption), the QDCB restricted its operations to commercial banks and the government.

The QDCB was not able to perform the function of banker to the government and commercial banks. The commercial banks, for example, only served as intermediaries between the board and the private sector. The QDCB was, therefore, essentially an automatic money-changer with no powers regarding monetary policy and general control over the financial/banking system in either Qatar or Dubai.

With the currency board powerless to influence liquidity in the country, flexibility in the Qatari financial system was introduced only by the local commercial banks, which were mostly branches of banks in the metropolitan country (UK).

After the establishment of the Qatar-Dubai Currency Board, by the signing of a currency agreement between Qatar and Dubai on 21 March 1966, the issuing of the Qatar-Dubai riyal was not immediate.

The devaluation of the Gulf rupee, to which the riyal was tied in June 1966, caused the introduction of the new currency to be postponed until 18 September 1966. In the six-month interim, the QDCB borrowed 100 million Saudi Arabian riyals for circulation in the two member countries, in place of the Gulf rupee.

The issue of the Qatar-Dubai riyal valued at 0.186621 grammes of fine gold (i.e. at par with the pre-devaluation Gulf rupee) was important not only for Qatar and Dubai. It was also an issue for Bahrain, Oman and the sheikhdoms comprising the United Arab Emirates with the exception of Abu Dhabi – where the Qatar-Dubai riyal became the sole legal tender currency for some time.

Commercial banking in Qatar during the pre-Qatar Monetary Board era was dominated by Britsh owned commercial banks. The main concentration of operations of these banks was in the financing of foreign trade, with their lending and investment policies determined by their head offices in Britain.

---

[1] El Mallakh, Ragaei. *Qatar: Development of an Oil Economy.* Croom Helm, London and St Martin's Press, New York 1979
El Mallakh, Ragaei. *Qatar: Energy and Development.* Croom Helm, London 1985

The effect was that even with demand or time deposits, no central monetary institution in Qatar wielded control over the local banks. Coupled with the passive activities of the Qatar-Dubai Currency Board there was virtually no monetary policy.

The Qatar-Dubai currency system was the first time the issue of currency was centralised in the two entities, yet the amount of money which circulated in Qatar continued to be determined by the balance of payments, to the extent that 100 per cent reserve banking was required.

On 13 May 1973, the Qatar Monetary Agency (QMA) was established by royal decree.

Even with the advent of the Qatar Monetary Agency it cannot be said that monetary policy in Qatar was completely independent of its balance of payments, which it was initially intended to be.

Fiscal policies could be tailored in such a way that some of the balance of payments effects were neutralised. In any case, the currency board system served as a stepping-stone to the establishment of a fully-fledged central banking system.

It was believed that control of the credit activities of commercial banks in Qatar during the currency board period were not necessary as long as the banking practices of the British commercial banks were not contrary to the interests of Qatar.

It was not until other foreign banks entered the picture by opening branches in Qatar that the emergence of divergent banking practices necessitated the establishment of a central monetary agency charged with the duty of providing a unifying direction for the banking system.

This chapter relies heavily on Appendices 5.1 to 5.5 which provide the background data needed to analyse how the QDCB evolved. They provide the appropriate financial statements which are then combined with the author's analysis.

Appendix 5.1 provides details of the Qatar Currency Law which enabled the creation of the QDCB.

Appendix 5.2 provides the financial statements of the Qatar Currency Board.

Appendix 5.3 contains the Annual Reports of the Qatar Currency Board. These form the basis for analysing the performance of the currency board.

Appendix 5.4 provides details of the author's calculations as to whether the Qatar Currency Board was, or was not, orthodox.

Appendix 5.5 provides the details of the Qatar Monetary Agency Law.

Methodological issues affecting monetary growth in the Qatar and Dubai Currency Board - Accounting Principles

The interpretation and tests of the performance of currency boards/agencies in the Gulf revolve around analysis of their accounting statements. Unfortunately, the presentation of currency board accounts was rarely straightforward. Profits and losses were often not clearly defined, nor was the rationale for the flows between the individual accounts. In addition, the same accounting conventions were not used for all the boards.

Accounting arrangements for the Qatar and Dubai Currency Board differed from most other boards in that a major liability, the currency in circulation, circulated for many years in both Qatar and Dubai. In addition the Dubai currency circulation overlapped with that of Bahrain. This is highlighted in Appendix 5.1.

This section outlines the flow of funds for the Qatar and Dubai Currency Board in order to get some feel for the performance of the board.

There are three accounts set out in the Qatar and Dubai Currency Board accounts:

1. Currency Issued Account (CIA)

Debits would occur if redemptions were greater than currency issues, and vice versa.

2. Balance Sheet (BS) and Currency Reserve Fund (CRF)

The BS and CRF are shown in one account, the BS. As these two accounts reveal different information it is still useful to discuss them separately. This account is designed to show the net worth of the board.

A balance sheet must balance hence the accounting principle here is:
Debits (liabilities) = Credits (assets).

The Currency Reserve Fund (CRF) account highlights the asset backing for the currency in circulation. This is essential for testing currency board orthodoxy.

Factors affecting the CRF are:

- Credits including gold reserves.
- Securities of foreign governments at cost.
- Treasury bills and cash.

A positive balance for the CRF means that foreign reserves are greater than the monetary liabilities.

This is one of the key characteristics of an orthodox currency board.

3. Currency Fund Income Account (CFIA)

This account illustrates whether the activities of the currency board are profitable or unprofitable. The accounting principle here is:

Debits > Credits = debit item in the CRF

Debits < Credits = credit item in the CRF

Box 5.1 below summarises these relationships.

Box 5.1 The tests for currency board orthodoxy

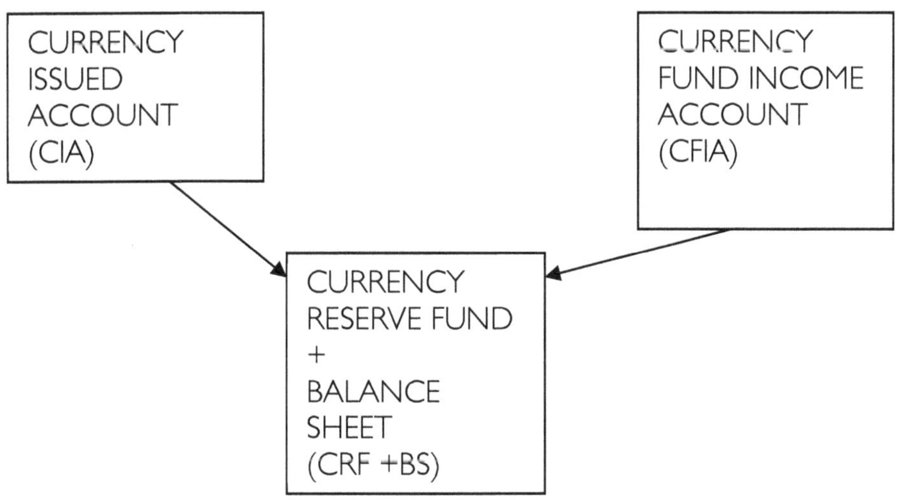

As can be seen from Table 5.1 the CIA grew dramatically in this period after falling somewhat between 1966 and 1969 due to the currency also circulating widely in Dubai.

The period from 1970-1972 was when oil reserves started feeding through. The BS and CRF accounts grew dramatically, reflecting the overall economic growth of Qatar. The CFIA data grew dramatically from 1966-1969. CFIA data was not available for the later years.

Table 5.1 Qatar-Dubai Currency Board Accounts 1966-1972

QDR, 000	1966	1967	1968	1969	1970	1971	1972
1.CIA	89,803,089	71,016,544	55,290,000	53,000,000	152,097,531	174,597,531	232,097,559
2.BS + CRF	86,589,099	131,619,452	154,805,364	170,035,148	178,395,269	200,917,174	249,854,118
3.CFIA	101,790	877,438	7,271,625	8,871,279			

Source: Qatar and Dubai Currency Board Reports

The Qatar Monetary Agency Era

The currency board system ultimately became too restrictive. In Qatar the oil boom in the 1970s made the establishment of a separate central monetary authority imperative. On 19 May 1973 the Qatar Monetary Agency (QMA) was established by royal decree.

The purpose of establishing the QMA was clearly stated in the 1973 law. See Appendix 5.5 for details of the law.

The QMA was established in accordance with the provisions of Law No. 7 (1973). That Law gave the QMA the traditional powers of a fully-fledged central bank. These powers included the issue and redemption of currency, safeguarding the internal and external value of the Qatari riyal, promotion of credit and exchange conditions conducive to economic growth and monetary stability, and the monitoring of banks and the financial system.

The QMA Law stipulated that the agency must maintain a reserve of external assets equal to 100 per cent of the currency in circulation (both notes and coins).

The QMA was responsible for regulating, redeeming and supplying currency, the Qatar riyal. It was also charged with the duty of ensuring both the internal and external stability of the riyal and safeguarding its convertibility into other currencies.

Another objective was to 'promote credit and exchange conditions conducive to the growth of the economy within the framework of monetary stability', and lastly the QMA had a supervisory power over the banks in Qatar. [8]

It should be noted that these functions of the QMA did not include explicitly serving as the banker to the government, nor as the banker's bank. Nonetheless, it did not allow that the functions could not be performed. Indeed, the functions of safeguarding the external and internal value of the riyal, ensuring its convertibility and promoting credit and exchange conditions favourable to development could be formed efficiently only if the commercial banks credit operations could be controlled and if the QMA held government credit instruments.

The broad manner in which the functions of the QMA were specified in the 1973 law was an indication of the flexibility given to the monetary authority in its attempts to exert control over the Qatar monetary system. See Appendix 5.1 for details of the QMA Law

It was not only the development-oriented nature of the functions of the QMA which made it a member of the emerging group of central banks for developing nations. Its close relationship with and almost complete control by the government of Qatar constituted a break with the older version of central banking legislation. The QMA was completely owned by the government of Qatar, and all the seven members of the board of directors were appointed by the Emir, upon the recommendation of the Minister of Finance.

Let us now turn to as to how and whether the Qatar currency board met the orthodoxy tests.

The Board of Directors of the QMA, consisting of the Governor, the Deputy Governor and five members, could define as external assets any or all of the following:

- gold coin or bullion;
- Special Drawing Rights and Qatar's gold tranche in the International Monetary Fund;
- convertible foreign currencies;
- bills of exchange, promissory notes;
- treasury bills and government (or government guaranteed) securities denominated in convertible foreign currencies.

The percentage of the currency cover could be changed by the Board of Directors of the QMA, with the approval of the Minister of Finance and Petroleum, for a period not exceeding six months.

Tests for the QDCA Currency orthodoxy are discussed below.

Testing for currency board authority orthodoxy

At least three tests of currency board orthodoxy are available:

(1) The ratio of authorised currency backing to currency in circulation. (ACB/CIC)
(2) The ratio of net foreign assets to reserve money. (NFA/RM)
(3) The ratio of net foreign assets to currency outside banks. (NFA/COB/CIC)

Appendix 5.4 provides data for a variety of tests of orthodoxy and liquidity undertaken by the Author.

The Qatar-Dubai Currency Board and the IMF's International Financial Statistics (IFS)

Qatar is listed under Qatar in IFS rather than Qatar-Dubai. However, Qatar was the dominant partner in the Qatar-Dubai Currency Board.

Testing for the orthodoxy of a currency board involves designing the appropriate tests and then deciding which monetary aggregates need to be applied to these tests. Monetary data can differ depending on the source.

It is useful to compare the differences between purely domestically generated data and that created by an outside body, in this case the IMF.

Organisations create data for differing purposes and it can be instructional to compare the outcome of the currency board tests given the differences in the data definitions.

As mentioned earlier at least three tests of currency board orthodoxy are available, the ratio of authorised currency backing to currency in circulation, the ratio of net foreign assets to reserve money and finally the ratio of net foreign assets to currency outside banks.

In undertaking and evaluating these tests it is obviously essential to try and compare like with like. For example, is the IMF's definition of Reserve Money the same concept as the currency liabilities of the currency board? Do the IMF's statistics on net foreign assets coincide with those of the currency board?

Many of these definitional issues are discussed in Chapter 6.

Are calculations on the ratio of net foreign assets to reserve money, based on IMF statistics, the same as those with the statistics from currency board reports concerning the ratio of the board's foreign investments to currency board liabilities?

Given that IFS definitions differ somewhat from standard country definitions of financial aggregates it is necessary to set out the IFS definitional position.

The IMF definitions as applied to (IFS) and relevant to the Qatar-Dubai Currency Board are defined throughout and are available in more detail. [2, 3]

In addition to testing for currency board orthodoxy analysis of the IFS data this also enables one to gain a better understanding of other monetary and banking developments during the currency board period.

As discussed in Chapter 4 an orthodox currency board has to have, as a minimum, net foreign assets to cover the whole of reserve money/monetary base. The terms 'reserve money' and the 'monetary base' are traditionally used interchangeably.

The IMF's terminology typically uses the monetary base defined as having the following components: currency in circulation outside of the central bank plus banks' deposits at the central bank and other private sector (demand) deposits at the central bank.

Using the IFS data for testing the ratio of net foreign assets to reserve money, the monetary base and additional tests mentioned above regarding currency orthodoxy becomes possible. One can also test the ratio of net foreign assets to currency outside banks, defined below. Currency held outside deposit money banks (DMBs) is traditionally referred to as 'currency in circulation'.

There may potentially be a large difference between reserve money and currency in circulation. The former includes, in addition to currency outside the central bank, deposits of commercial banks at the central bank (required and excess reserves) and in some countries also includes non-bank private sector deposits.

Also, the currency component of reserve money includes currency held by commercial banks. The holdings in this latter element are usually excluded from currency in circulation data which is designed to capture notes and coins in the hands of the non-bank private sector.

A more powerful test for currency board orthodoxy is that Net Foreign Assets (NFA) cover Reserve Money although tests for the extent to which NFA covers currency held outside deposit money banks are also undertaken by the author. See Figures 5.7 and 5.8.

These latter tests enable a better understanding of the extent to which the currency in circulation component of the monetary base is covered by external assets

Qatar joined the International Monetary Fund on 8 September 1972 and the earliest recorded IFS data is for 1966. Hence data for the majority of the currency board period, 1966-1973, can be found in International Financial Statistics (IFS) usefully enabling the various tests of the performance of the currency board undertaken by the author.

Testing for Currency Board Orthodoxy

Figure 5.1 shows that the board's balance sheet grew rapidly during the currency board period with assets growing more quickly than liabilities

Figure 5.1 Balance Sheet Statement 1966-1972

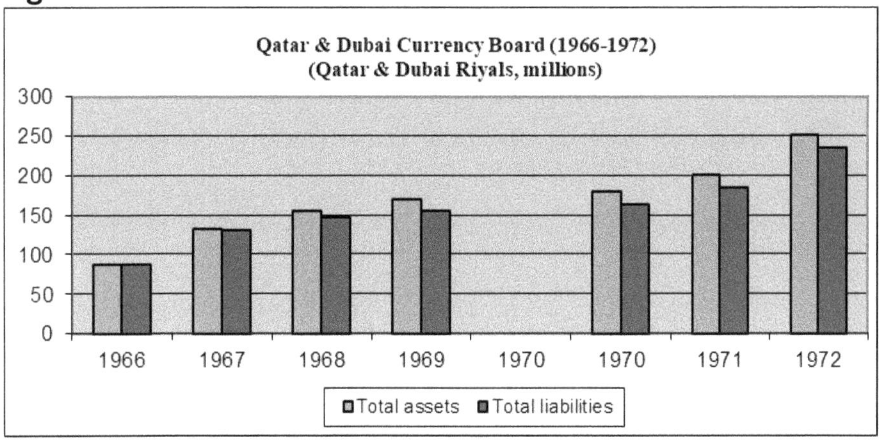

Source: Annual Reports of the Qatar & Dubai Currency Board

As can be seen from Figure 5. 2 income grew rapidly during the currency board period with income falling back slightly towards the end, but still substantially more than expenditures.

Figure 5.2 Income and Expenditure Statement

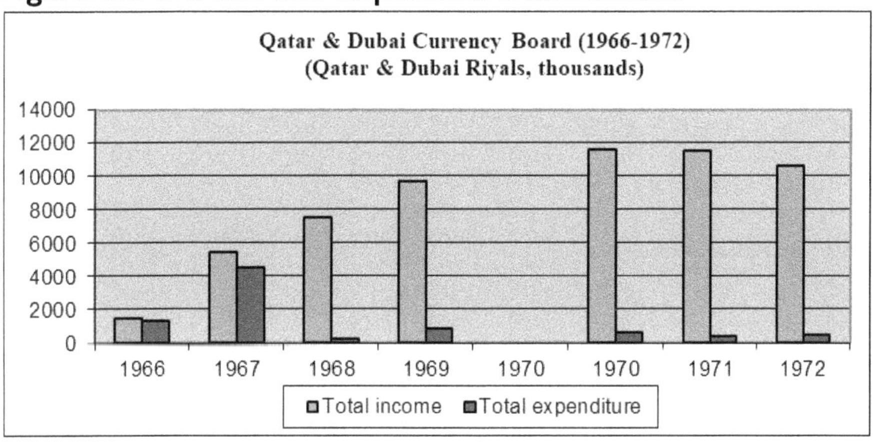

Source: Annual Reports of the Qatar and Dubai Currency Board

Figure 5.3 highlights that the authorised currency backing either covered, or was equal to, currency in circulation during the currency board period, albeit falling back in 1972. This indicates that the orthodoxy tests were being met.

ORTHODOXY TEST 1 (ACB /CIC)

Figure 5.3 Currency Backing Analysis 1966-1972

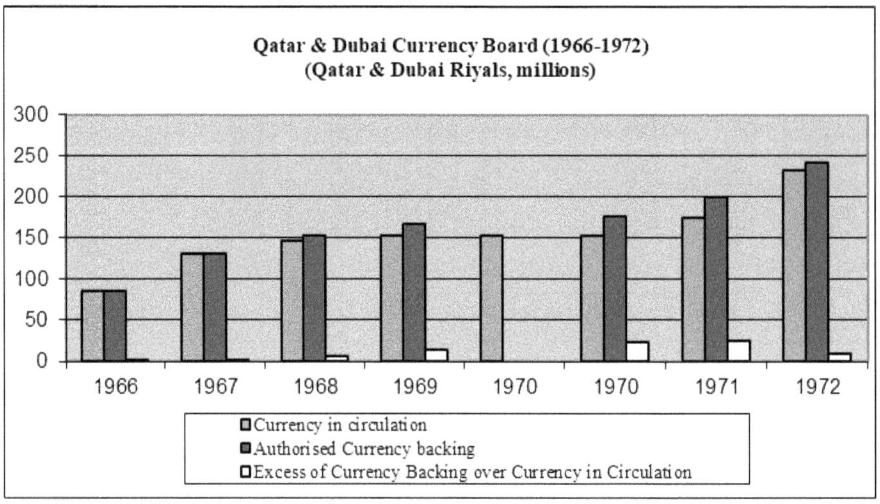

Source: Annual Reports of the Qatar and Dubai Currency Board
(Author's calculations)

Figure 5.4 illustrates a key orthodoxy test (100 per cent) illustrating that the orthodoxy test was met, with some years overperforming considerably in 1969, 1970, 1971 and 1972.

Figure 5.4 Test for Orthodoxy 1966-1972 (per cent)

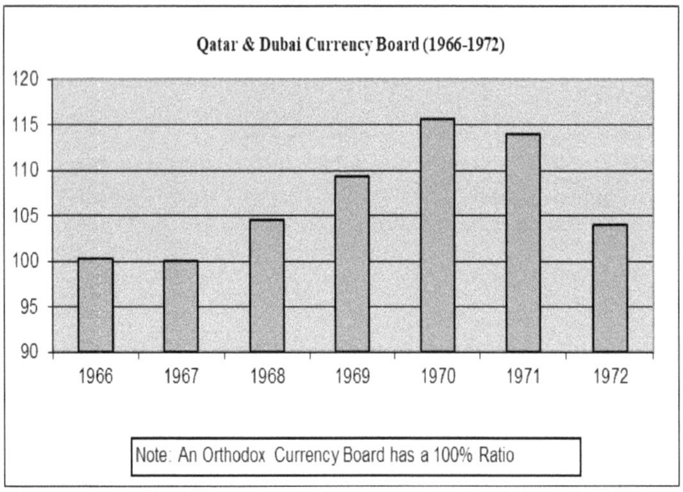

Source: Annual Reports of the Qatar and Dubai Currency Board
(Author's calculations)

As can be seen from Figure 5.5, total liquid external assets and total external assets grew faster than Currency in Circulation during the period. This again illustrates that the board was orthodox.

Figure 5.5 Composition and Degree of Liquidity of Assets 1966-1972

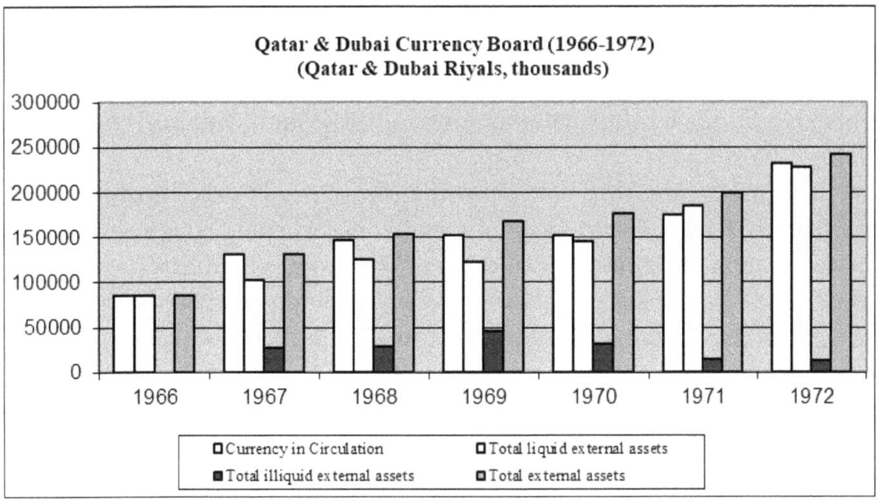

Source: Annual Reports of the Qatar and Dubai Currency Board
(Author's calculations)

Figure 5.6 highlights that liquid assets as a percentage of external assets during the period, varied between 68 per cent and 100 per cent meaning the board provided adequate liquidity for it to be considered an orthodox currency board.

Figure 5.6 Liquid and Illiquid External Assets as a Percentage of Total External Assets 1966-1972 (per cent)

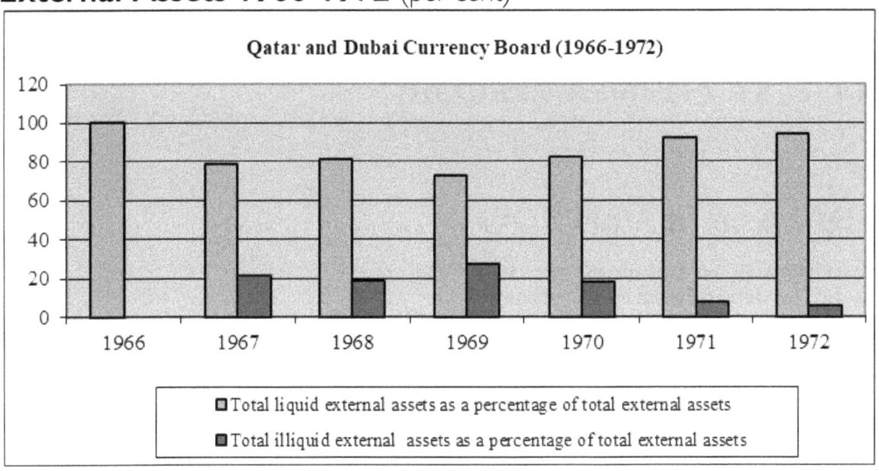

Source: Annual Reports of the Qatar-Dubai Currency Board 1965-1973
(Author's calculations)

The Qatar-Dubai Currency Board and the IMF's International Financial Statistics (IFS)

How do these orthodoxy findings differ when comparing IMF data with currency board data?

As can be seen from Figure 5.7 the IMF data show that the Qatar-Dubai Currency Board was more orthodox than that using Qatar-Dubai Currency Board data. To appreciate why this is the case it is necessary, as mentioned earlier, to look at some definitions.

Unfortunately, the Qatar-Dubai Currency Board did not provide detailed definitions so one is obliged to rely on the face value of the items, mentioned in the actual currency board reports, as being what they purport to measure.

The reason why IMF findings differ is due to either the IMF using a wider definition of reserve assets or a narrower definition of monetary liabilities, or both, than those of the currency board definitions.

As can be seen below the IMF definitions of foreign reserves, and with them net foreign assets, frequently include, under 'monetary authorities' some activities of government treasuries or ministries of finance or other official agencies that are extra to the holdings by the currency boards.

In other words, the IMF definition captures some of the consolidated reserves of other government agencies. In practice the IMF money supply definitions are usually at least as broad as those of national measures.

As can be seen from Figures 5.7 and 5.8 using a variety of monetary criteria the orthodoxy tests were met.

Figure 5.7 shows the data test for orthodoxy using the size of net foreign assets, reserve money and currency outside banks. Orthodoxy tests were being met with all the criteria.

ORTHODOXY TEST 2 /3 (NFA/RM/COB)

Figure 5.7 IMF DATA on NFA/RM/COBs

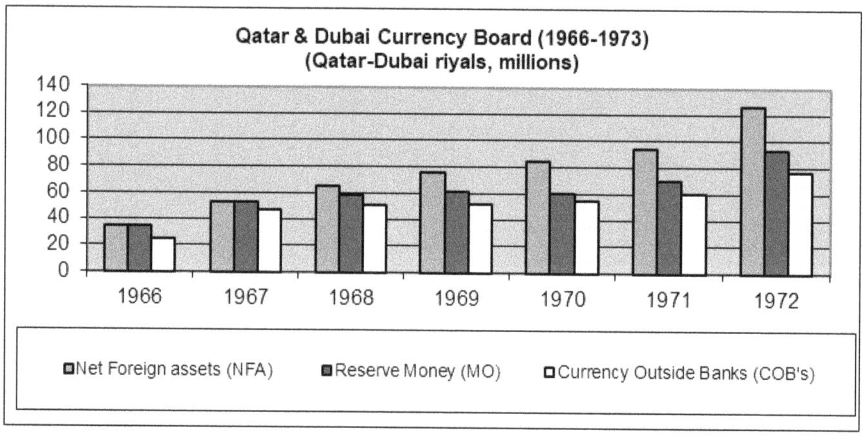

Source: International Financial Statistics, IMF (Author.s calculations)

Figure 5.8 illustrates that using the test for orthodoxy using the ratios of Net Foreign Assets to MO and to NFA to currency outside deposit money banks, that orthodoxy tests were met for all the criteria.

Figure 5.8 Tests of Currency Board Orthodoxy applying IMF data 1966-1972 (per cent)

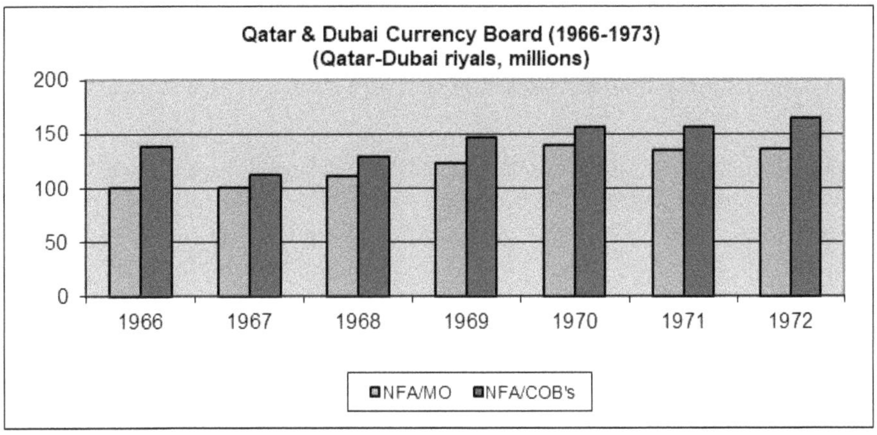

Source IFS ***(Author's calculations)***

SELECTED REFERENCES

[1]Appendices 1 to 4 provide detailed breakdowns of the Middle East and Gulf currency arrangements for the relevant periods for this text.
[2]*IMF Monetary and Financial Statistics Manual,* pp325-330 2000.
[3]*IMF System of National Accounts. IMF Balance of Payments Manual (Fifth edition)* 1993
Schuler, Kurt. *Currency Boards. A [Doctoral] Dissertation.* George Mason University, Fairfax, Virginia 1992.
For a more complete discussion of currency boards see the above thesis which this section draws upon.

Appendix 5.1

The Qatar-Dubai Currency Authority (QDCA)

Interestingly the opening section of the official agreement draws attention to the breakdown of the Arabian Gulf Currency Agreement, which was designed to introduce a common currency into some of the Gulf States agreed to the introduction of the Qatar-Dubai currency Board:

> 'The Arabian Gulf Currency Agreement signed at Dubai on the ninth day of Rabi' al-Awwal 1385, corresponding to 7 July 1965, concluded between the States of Bahrain, Qatar, Abu Dhabi, and Dubai has encountered obstacles which have hindered its enforcement.
>
> 'And considering that the Governments of Qatar and Dubai are moved by the joint desire to expedite on introducing a common currency to replace the Indian and other currencies now in circulation.
>
> 'And desiring to constitute a currency authority to issue and manage this common currency in the two States and in other countries of the Arabian Gulf which accept the authority's currency as sole legal tender for them in compliance with the conditions and terms which may be agreed upon between the concerned parties.'

The key articles of this agreement are listed below.

Article 2

There shall be established from the two Participating Governments a Currency Authority to be known as the Qatar and Dubai Currency Authority.

Article 3

The objects of the Authority shall be to issue legal tender currency in accordance with the provisions of this Agreement and to maintain external reserves in order to safeguard the international value of that currency.

Article 19

The unit of currency shall be the Qatar and Dubai Riyal with a parity of 0.186621 grammes of fine gold. The Qatar and Dubai Riyal shall be divided into one hundred equal units, each of which shall be called one dirham.

Article 23

Subject to any requirements existing at any time pertaining to Exchange Control within the Currency Area, the Authority shall, through its agents, on demand, issue currency in the Currency Area against payment in sterling in London. Such issue shall be at the rate of one Qatar and Dubai Riyal for one and a half shillings sterling provided that the

Authority may charge a commission at the rate from time to time fixed by it. This commission shall not in any case exceed one per cent.

Article 26

The Authority shall: -

a) establish a Currency Reserve Fund, to which each of the two Participating Governments shall pay a sum in sterling equivalent to the amount of the existing currency withdrawn from circulation in its territory, and the Fund shall be maintained so that the value of its assets as defined in Article (29) of this Agreement, shall not be less than the value of currency in circulation;

b) credit the Currency Reserve Fund with sterling received for the issue of notes and coins, and with such other amounts as may be stipulated in this Agreement; and debit the Currency Reserve Fund with payments made in sterling for the redemption of notes and coins.

Article 27

Each of the two Participating Governments shall pay to the Authority for credit to the Currency Reserve Fund a sum in sterling as set out below: -

A sum equivalent to the total value of the existing currency withdrawn from circulation in its territory during the period prescribed under Article 43 (a) of this Agreement. Such payment shall be made in the following manner: -

i) at the request of the Authority an initial payment:

   a) by the Government of Qatar of six million pounds (£6 million).
   b) by the Government of Dubai of two and a half million pounds (£2.5 million).

Article 28

When all payments due under Article (27) have been made, any of the two Participating Governments which regards the total amount it has paid to the Currency Reserve Fund under Article (27) as disproportionately large (through any abnormal rise in the amount of the existing currency withdrawn in its territory at the time of withdrawal) may request the Board to review the position in the light of the evidence available. The Board may make such recommendations as it may think fit, and the two Participating Governments shall use their best endeavours to give effect to the Authority's recommendations.

Article 29

The assets of the Currency Reserve Fund shall consist only of the following: -

a) gold coins and bullion;

b) cash, or money at call, in sterling or other currencies freely convertible into gold or sterling;

c) Treasury bills of foreign Governments expressed in sterling or in other currencies freely convertible into gold or sterling, with a maturity of not more than 93 days;

d) securities of, or guaranteed by, foreign Governments and expressed in sterling or in other currencies freely convertible into gold or sterling, provided that such securities maturing in more than five years from the date of purchase shall not exceed 20 per cent of the total assets of the Fund;

e) the existing currency for such period as the Authority may prescribe.

Article 30

The Authority shall: -

a) establish a Currency Fund Income Account, which shall be credited with all the revenue of the Authority and such other amounts as maybe stipulated in this Agreement, and which shall be debited with all expenditure incurred by the Authority;

b) transfer at the end of each financial year, after provision for all contingencies, any surplus on the Currency Fund Income Account to the Currency Reserve Fund.

Article 34

After the close of each financial year, the net surplus in the Authority's Currency Fund Income as certified by the auditors shall, after providing for all contingencies, be transferred to the Currency Reserve Fund.

Article 35

Should the Authority find at the close of any financial year, and after such transfer as is referred to in the previous Article has been effected, that the Currency Reserve Fund is insufficient to one hundred per cent cover the currency then in issue the two Participating Governments shall forthwith, and in the proportions calculated in accordance with Article (37) of this Agreement, make good such deficiency and each Participating Government shall regard its share of the amount required as a first charge on its General Revenues.

Article 36

Should the Authority be satisfied at the close of any financial year that the Currency Reserve Fund is sufficient to guarantee the redemption of currency notes and coins not less than one hundred per cent, and contains in addition assets equivalent in value to not less than ten per cent of the value of currency circulation, it shall pay any excess amount to the two Participating Governments in the proportions calculated in accordance with Article (37) of this Agreement.

Article 37

Except as may be otherwise agreed by the two Participating Governments, any payments made under Articles (35) and (36) of this Agreement shall be such that the share of a Participating Government in the full amount of the Payment shall bear the same proportion to such amount as the Participating Government's payment to the Currency Reserve Fund made under Article (27) (after taking account of adjustments, if any, made under Article (28) of this Agreement) bears to the total payments made by the two Participating Governments to that Fund. This proportion shall be expressed as a percentage (to the nearest unit) of the total, and shall apply to payments due under Article (35) from, or to be received under Article (36) by the two Participating Governments, until such time as the two Participating Governments, on the unanimous recommendation of the Authority, agree to different proportions.

Article 43

a) Every holder of the existing currency shall have the right to exchange it for the new currency at a rate based on the parity value of the Qatar and Dubai Riyal, as defined in Article (19) of this Agreement, for a period commencing on the Appointed Day and terminating on a date fixed by the Decree which establishes the Appointed Day.

b) The Authority may, if it thinks fit, exchange the existing currency for the new currency after the expiry of the said period. Thereafter currencies other than the new currency shall cease to be legal tender in the Currency Area.

Article 51

The two Participating Governments undertake to give legal effect to the provisions of this Agreement by each enacting a Decree not later than the 29th Zil Hijja of year 1385 (H) (corresponding to the twentieth day of April 1966) to be brought into force with effect from that date:

Done at Doha this 29th day of Zil Qida 1385, corresponding to 21 March 1966.

Appendix 5.2 Qatar and Dubai Board Financia; Statements 1966-1972

Table 5.2a Balance Sheet Statement Qatar-Dubai Riyals 1966-1969

1 Balance Sheet Statement				
(Qatar- Dubai Riyals, as at 31st December)				
1 QDR= 0.075 Sterling				
ASSETS	**1966**	**1967**	**1968**	**1969**
Gold		23,160,021	30,833,513	30,833,513
British Government securities		27,884,285	28,348,214	45,438,035
British Government Treasury Bills	26,888,566	73,041,974	51,313,046	47,363,313
Cash with foreign banks on deposit and current account	58,760,269	6,632,267	42,795,477	43,616,360
Cash with local banks		72,887	16,631	53,498
Interest due but not received	940,273	828,015	1,494,331	2,727,527
Sundry debtors			4,150	2,900
Compensation under Basle Facility				
1.1 Total assets	**86,589,108**	**131,619,449**	**154,805,362**	**170,035,146**
LIABILITIES				
Currency Reserve Fund				
Currency in circulation	85,466,306	130,632,973	146,547,259	152,897,514
Amount due to Government of Qatar	1,003,237			
Sundry creditors	17,765	7,250	7,250	1,847,882
1.2 Total liabilities	**86,487,308**	**130,640,223**	**146,554,509**	**154,745,396**
Special reserve account	101,790	979,229	8,250,855	15,289,751
Total liabilities and reserve account	86,589,098	131,619,452	154,805,364	170,035,147
2 Income and Expenditure Statement				
INCOME	**1966**	**1967**	**1968**	**1969**
Profits on sale of securities		172,938	273,571	510,892

Discount on Treasury Bills	53,784	3,740,392	3,637,452	3,113,890
Interest on securities		669,714	1,281,839	2,749,788
Interest on bank deposits	1,282,325	415,890		
Interest on money employed	85,298	288,931	270,959	263,884
Interest on foreign currency deposits			1,358,439	2,930,399
Commissions on issues and redemptions	22,841	121,041	118,107	124,562
Revaluation of foreign currency assets			545,601	
2.1 Total income	**1,444,248**	**5,408,906**	**7,485,968**	**9,693,415**
EXPENDITURE				
	1,286,296	477,059	18,277	266,923
Fees of Members of the Board	3,379	18,656	24,719	23,422
Staff salaries	24,980	82,703	94,790	106,394
Currency agents' fees	4,000	5,369	23,506	37,959
Auditors' fees	5,000	7,000	7,250	15,500
Administrative expenses	18,801	74,268	34,840	37,219
Adjustment of purchase price of gold to parity		152,470	10,962	
Depreciation in value of securities		236,250		
Revaluation of foreign currency assets		3,477,692		334,718
2.2 Total expenditure	**1,342,456**	**4,531,467**	**214,344**	**822,135**
2.3 Balance being transferred to Special Reserve Account	101,790	877,438	7,271,625	8,871,279
2.4 Total expenditure plus reserve	1,444,246	5,408,905	7,485,969	9,693,414
Source: Annual Reports of the Qatar Dubai Currency Board				

Table 5.2b Balance Sheet Statement Qatar-Dubai Riyals 1970-1972

1 Balance Sheet Statement			
(Qatar- Dubai Riyals, as at 31st December)			
1 QDR= 0.075 Sterling			
ASSETS	**1970**	**1971**	**1972**
Gold	30,833,513	30,833,513	30,833,513
British Government securities	31,255,892	14,627,321	13,181,329
British Government Treasury Bills	55,014,021	96,868,311	136,935,041
Cash with foreign banks on deposit and current account	58,836,434	56,737,196	60,397,705
Cash with local banks	55,419	76,563	3,648,405
Interest due but not received	2,398,338	1,767,468	2,085,616
Sundry debtors	1,650	6,800	
Compensation under Basle Facility			2,772,507
1.1 Total assets	**178,395,267**	**200,917,172**	**249,854,116**
LIABILITIES			
Currency Reserve Fund			
Currency in circulation	152,097,531	174,597,531	232,097,559
Amount due to Government of Qatar	11,073,985	8,840,157	
Sundry creditors	14,000	19,733	2,083,100
1.2 Total liabilities	**163,185,516**	**183,457,421**	**234,180,659**
Special reserve account	15,209,753	17,459,753	15,673,459
Total liabilities and reserve account	178,395,269	200,917,174	249,854,118
2 Income and Expenditure Statement			
INCOME	**1970**	**1971**	**1972**

Profits on sale of securities	868,297	514,285	
Discount on Treasury Bills	3,201,022	3,855,588	6,334,055
Interest on securities	2,992,916	1,804,931	922,342
Interest on bank deposits			
Interest on money employed	233,724	211,263	193,753
Interest on foreign currency deposits	4,012,770	3,328,649	1,926,834
Commissions on issues and redemptions	138,750	121,988	868,266
Revaluation of foreign currency assets	138,160	1,658,518	360,043
2.1 Total income	**11,585,639**	**11,495,222**	**10,605,293**
EXPENDITURE			
	103,496	71,254	192,458
Fees of Members of the Board	27,338	22,942	23,167
Staff salaries	148,862	141,725	96,717
Currency agents' fees	34,296	62,972	41,607
Auditors' fees	24,250	45,750	67,603
Administrative expenses	253,419	60,423	41,880
Adjustment of purchase price of gold to parity			
Depreciation in value of securities			
Revaluation of foreign currency assets			
2.2 Total expenditure	**591,661**	**405,066**	**463,432**
2.3 Balance being transferred to Special Reserve Account	10,993,987	11,090,157	10,141,862
2.4 Total expenditure plus reserve	11,585,648	11,495,223	10,605,294

Appendix 5.3

Qatar-Dubai Currency Board Annual Reports 1966-1972 [1 2]

First Annual Report for the Qatar-Dubai Currency Board 31 December 1966

(The currency board was based in Doha)

Following the delays in the implementation of the Arabian Gulf Currency Agreement, which was signed in July 1965 by the rulers of Qatar, Abu Dhabi and Bahrain, the rulers of Qatar and Dubai decided to proceed with arrangements for the replacement of the Gulf rupee, which had been in circulation in the area since 1959, with their own currency. The Qatar-Dubai Currency Agreement (QDCA) was accordingly signed on 21 March, 1966.

The Agreement stipulated that the new currency unit should be the Qatar and Dubai riyal with the parity of 0.186621 grammes of fine gold, equivalent to 1½ shillings sterling and that the riyal should be divided into 100 dirhams. It further provided for the establishment of a currency board to manage the currency and lay down that there should be a Currency Reserve Fund consisting of specified foreign exchange assets to a total value no less than that of the currency in circulation. The agreement requires that the currency board shall issue and redeem the currency against the transfer of sterling in London.

Following the signing of the agreement (QDCA), the devaluation of the Indian rupee on 6 June 1966 took place before the new currency could be introduced. In order to protect their countries from the ill effects of that devaluation which, despite their protests, affected the Gulf rupee, the rulers of Qatar and Dubai requested the banks to conduct business in Gulf rupees at pre-devaluation rates. For technical reasons it was decided to withdraw the Gulf rupees from circulation as soon as possible and the government of Qatar, with the co-operation of the Saudi Arabian Monetary Agency, accordingly arranged to borrow notes totalling 100 million Saudi Arabian riyals against the collateral of sterling deposits in London.

Saudi riyal notes were put into circulation at the end of June 1966 and at the same time the Gulf rupee was withdrawn. The rate of exchange applied was 106.5 Gulf rupees for 100 Saudi Arabian riyals and thereafter Gulf rupee notes ceased to be legal tender.

On 31 August, 1966 the Qatar-Dubai Currency Agreement was ended to the extent that references to the Gulf rupee as the existing currency were replaced by references to Saudi Arabian riyals, whose owners were therefore given the right to exchange them at par into the new currency.

By the middle of September 1966 sufficient quantities of Qatar and Dubai notes and lower denomination coins had been received from Bradbury's, Wilkinson & Company Limited and the Royal Mint respectively.

The exchange of new currency in exchange for Saudi Arabian notes and coins (in Qatar) and Bahraini coins (in Dubai) began in mid-September and continued for four days.

The banks in Qatar were further authorised to continue the exchange of Saudi Arabian notes for another three weeks at the same rate of exchange, i.e. 106.5 Qatar and Dubai riyals for 100 Saudi Arabian riyals.

The total value of Qatar and Dubai currency put into circulation during the exchange operation amounted to 74,859,640 Qatar and Dubai riyals of which 73,944,065 Qatar and Dubai riyals represented notes and 915,575 Qatar and Dubai riyals coins. The sterling equivalent, namely £5,614,473, was paid to the currency board by the government of Qatar, in the form of sterling deposits with banks in London. As the entire cover for the currency was provided by the government of Qatar, the two governments signed, on 29 October 1966, an agreement to the effect that the government of Qatar would be solely responsible for any deficiencies in the Currency Reserve Fund, under Article 35 of the Currency Agreement, and would also be solely entitled to all profits under Article 36 of the Agreement.

The total income of the currency board up to 31 December 1966 was 1,444,251/10 QD riyals (including the accrued interest referred to above), and this amount exceeded expenditure by 101,790/61 QD riyals, which, in accordance with Article 34 of the currency agreement, was credited to a Special Reserve Account.

Annual Report for the Qatar–Dubai Currency Board 31 December 1967

The second year of the Qatar and Dubai Currency Board was heavily influenced by the devaluation of sterling on 18 November 1967, by about 14.3 per cent

As the Gulf states concerned had already undertaken two currency changes within the previous eighteen months, it seemed particularly important at that time that there should be no loss of confidence in the local currency. It was also necessary, of course, to avoid, if possible, any adverse effects which would have resulted from an alteration in the purchasing power of the Qatar and Dubai riyal.

The governments of Qatar and Dubai therefore decided that there should be no change in the gold value of the Qatar and Dubai riyal, as laid down in Article 19 of the Qatar-Dubai Currency Agreement, and that its value in terms of sterling should be increased from one and half shillings sterling to one and three quarter shillings sterling, i.e. to one shilling and nine pence. Article 23 of the currency agreement was amended accordingly by an agreement dated 27 November 1967.

In the light of the above decision, it became necessary to revalue the sterling assets held by the currency board as at 19 November, 1967, and the resultant loss, namely 14,906,264/02 QD riyals, was made good by a payment of £1,000,000 (11,428,571/43 QD riyals) to the currency board by the government of Qatar and by debiting the balance (3,477,692/59 QD riyals) to the Currency Fund Income Account.

During 1967 the currency in circulation in Qatar and Dubai increased by 45,166,666/67 QD riyals and at the end of December stood at 130,632,973/34 QD riyals – a rise of about 53 per cent over the year.

By the end of 1967 the Qatar and Dubai riyal had established itself as the main currency in Sharjah, Ras Al Khaimah, Ajman, Fujairah and Umm Al Quwain as well as in Qatar and Dubai.

Annual Report for the Qatar–Dubai Currency Board 31 December 1968

Two decisions of importance were taken by the directors of the currency board in 1968 – the first in January when it was decided to diversify the board's assets by switching a proportion of its sterling holdings into other foreign currencies and the second in September when the Sterling Guarantee Agreement with the government of the United Kingdom was signed. At the end of 1967 about one fifth of the assets of the currency board was invested in gold and the remainder almost wholly in British government securities and treasury bills. Following the decision to diversify its holdings, in order to protect the reserves against the risk of further devaluation of sterling, the percentage of the board's assets in sterling was reduced to about 50 per cent by the end of July at which other foreign currencies (United States dollars and Swiss francs) accounted for about 28 per cent of external reserves and gold for 22 per cent.

The effect of the Sterling Guarantee Agreement, which had a three year duration on the lines of those arranged between other sterling area countries and the United Kingdom, was that in return for an undertaking by the board to maintain the existing proportion of sterling held in its external reserves, the British government guaranteed, in terms of US dollars, the bulk of the board's sterling holdings against the risk of a change in the sterling/dollar rate of exchange. This guarantee, it was argued, made it unnecessary therefore to further diversify the reserves and enabled the board to benefit from the high rates of interest prevailing in London without risk of loss should sterling be devalued in terms of the dollar.

During 1968 the currency in circulation in Qatar and Dubai increased by QDR15,914,285.72 and at the end of December stood at QDR146,547,259.06. This was a rise of only 12 per cent compared with an increase of over 50 per cent in 1967.

At the end of 1968, the currency board held gold to the value of QDR30,833,513.17 and short-dated British government securities and treasury bills to the value of QDR79,661,260.48. These assets represented 21.0 per cent and 54.4 per cent respectively of the currency in circulation. At the same time, cash with foreign banks on deposit and current accounts amounted to QDR42,795,477.71 and represented 29.2 per cent of the currency in circulation. As compared with the end of 1967 position, cash with foreign banks on deposit and current accounts increased considerably at the expense of short-dated securities and treasury bills. This was due to the fact that the board's US dollar and Swiss franc holdings were invested in time deposits with foreign banks.

The Currency Fund Income Account was credited on 31 December 1968 with the sum of QDR1,494,331.18, being the interest due but not received at that date on British government securities and treasury bills and money on time deposit with foreign banks. The income account showed a profit of QDR7,271,625.79 for the year ended 31 December 1968, and in accordance with Article 34 of the currency agreement, this amount was transferred to the Special Reserve Account, the balance on which then stood at QDR8,250,855.14 (5.6 per cent of the currency in circulation).

Annual Report for the Qatar–Dubai Currency Board 31 December 1969

The investment policy formulated by the currency board in 1968 continued during 1969. As the board's holdings of sterling were guaranteed in terms of US dollars under the Sterling Guarantee Agreement of September 1968 no switches from sterling were effected and the board's holding of gold and other currencies (US dollars and Swiss francs) were maintained. Thus, the whole impact of changes in total holdings of external assets arising from fluctuations in the currency in circulation was reflected in changes in the holdings of sterling. However, the fluctuations of total external assets moved only within narrow limits between a low of 53.6 per cent at the end of September and a high of 57.7 per cent at the end of December. Holdings of sterling were invested partly in treasury bills and partly in UK Government sterling securities maturing within the next two years. Working balances were maintained on current account with the Bank of England and in the form of money employed in the London money market.

The increase in the level of currency in circulation during 1969 was the smallest since the inception of the currency board. The total value in circulation at 31 December was QDR152,897,514.06 as against QDR146,547,259.06 a year earlier, a rise of only 4.3 per cent.

With the continuation of the board's previous investment policy there was no fundamental change in the composition of the board's assets. At the end of 1969 gold represented 20.2 per cent of the value of currency in circulation, while British government treasury bills and short-dated securities for 60.7 per cent. United States dollars and Swiss francs held with foreign banks amounted to 26.1 per cent.

The Currency Fund Income Account showed a profit of QDR8,871,279.147 for the year, which was transferred, in accordance with Article 34 of the Qatar-Dubai Currency Agreement, to the Currency Reserve Fund, making the balance on the Special Reserve Account QDR17,122,134.28. As the balance in the Currency Reserve Fund then exceeded 110 per cent of currency in circulation, the board decided to pay the excess, i.e. QDR1,832,382.87, to the government of Qatar in accordance with Articles 36 and 37 of the currency agreement. This payment is included in the balance sheet under sundry creditors.

Annual Report for the Qatar–Dubai Currency Board 31 December 1970

The strength of the Qatar-Dubai riyal, backed by holdings of external assets amounting to not less than 110 per cent of the currency in circulation continued to stimulate confidence which has been reflected in particular in a further increase in the volume of banking business in the currency area and in the expansion of the banking network.

Fluctuations in total external assets of the currency board were relatively low during the year under review and reflected the seasonal changes in the level of the currency in circulation. As the percentage of sterling in total external assets tended to rise gradually (to 57.9 per cent at March 1970) the bulk of the board's income being received in sterling, the board reviewed the distribution of its holdings and switched part of the accumulation of sterling into other currencies. By December 1970 the proportion of sterling in total external assets had fallen to 52.2 per cent and that of other currencies had risen to 30.3 per cent. The board's holdings of gold remained unchanged over the year.

Holdings of sterling were invested partly in treasury bills and partly in short-term British government sterling securities. Working balances were maintained on current account with the Bank of England and in the form of money employed in the London money market. Holdings of the other foreign currencies (US dollars, Swiss francs, and Deutsche Marks) were invested in time deposits with banks. The board's holdings of sterling continued to be guaranteed in terms of the US dollar under the Sterling Guarantee Agreement signed in September 1968.

The level of currency in circulation showed little change in 1970 over 1969. The total amount in circulation at 31 December being QDR152,097,531 against QDR152,897,514 in the same month in 1969, a fall of 0.5 per cent compared with a rise of 4.3 per cent in 1969.

The Currency Fund Income Account showed a profit of QDR10,993,987 as compared to QDR8,871,279 in the previous financial year. The increase in profit was due partly to the larger average holding of external assets and partly to the high interest rates, which prevailed over most of 1970 on the international money markets.

In accordance with Article 34 of the Qatar-Dubai Currency Agreement, the profit of QDR10,993,987 was transferred into the Currency Reserve Fund making the balance on the Special Reserve Account of QDR26,283,783. As, after the transfer, the balance on the Currency Reserve Fund exceeded 10 per cent of currency in circulation, the board decided to pay the excess, QDR11,073,985 to the government of Qatar in accordance with Articles 36 and 37 of the currency agreement.

Annual Report for the Qatar-Dubai Currency Board 31 December 1971

On 2 September 1971, Qatar achieved full independence as a sovereign state. Three months later, on 2 December 1971, Dubai achieved independence as a member of the United Arab Emirates. The activities of the currency board continued unchanged in both Qatar and Dubai.

Towards the end of 1970 the board decided gradually to switch its holdings of dollars into other currencies on maturity of the respective deposits. At the time of the devaluation of the US dollar in December 1971 no dollars were held by the board and apart from sterling the board was holding only deutschmarks and Swiss francs. Holdings of gold remained unchanged throughout the year. The proportion of sterling holdings in total external assets rose from 52.2 per cent at the end of 1970 to 56.9 per cent at the end of 1971. The Sterling Guarantee Agreement under which the value of the sterling holdings of the board was guaranteed in terms of the US dollar, was extended for another two years until September 1973.

Currency in circulation rose during 1971 by QDR22.5m or 14.8 per cent, as compared with a fall of 0.5 per cent in 1970 and an increase of only 4.3 per cent in 1969. At the end of December 1971 the circulation stood at a new all-time peak of QDR174,597,531.

The Currency Fund Income Account showed a profit of QDR11,090,157 compared to QDR10,993,987 in 1970 and QDR8,871,279 in 1969. The slight increase in profits in a period of falling interest rates on international money markets was due to higher average level of assets held by the board and to exchange profits on the board's holdings of deutschmarks and Swiss francs.

In accordance with Article 34 of the Qatar-Dubai Currency Agreement the profit of QDR11,090,157 had been transferred to the Currency Reserve Fund making the balance on the Special Reserve Account of QDR26,299,910 or 15.06 per cent of the currency in circulation.

In accordance with Articles 36 and 37 of the currency agreement the board decided to pay to the government of Qatar the excess over the mandatory 10 per cent of the currency in circulation amounting to QDR8,840,157.

Annual Report for the Qatar–Dubai Currency Board 31 December 1972

The depreciation of sterling following the announcement that, with effect from 23 June 1972, that sterling was to be allowed to float resulted in substantial losses on the board's holdings of that currency. The guarantee given by the British governmentunder the Sterling Guarantee Agreement concluded in September 1968, was expressed in terms of the US dollar and was to come into effect in case the sterling-dollar rate fell below US$2.40 for £1 sterling. The devaluation of the US dollar in December 1971 resulted in the sterling dollar rate moving to US dollars 2.6057. Thus, when in turn sterling depreciated, the board had no recourse to the British government until the rate fell below US$2.40 to the pound.

This actually took place in the second half of October and on 23' November 1972 the board became entitled to compensation under the Sterling Guarantee Agreement, based on the difference between the rate of US$2.40 stipulated in the agreement and the rate of US$2.3506, being the closing middle rate on 23 November. The amount of that compensation (QDR2,772.507), actually received in January 1973, has been included in the board's accounts for 1972, and helped to offset part of the loss on sterling holdings.

No changes were made in the board's investment policy. Holdings of gold and currencies other than sterling (Swiss francs and deutschmarks) were maintained throughout the year at the level prevailing at the end of 1971 and the impact of the change in total holdings of external assets rising from the considerable increase in the currency circulation was reflected in the rise of sterling holdings. The proportion of sterling in total external assets amounted to 64.8 per cent at the end of 1972 compared to 56.9 per cent a year earlier.

Currency in circulation rose during 1972 by QDR57.5m or 32.9 per cent as compared to the rise of 14.8 per cent in 1971 and the fall of 5 per cent in 1970. The circulation stood at QDR232,097.559 at the end of the year.

The Currency Fund Income Account showed a surplus of QDR10,141,862 as compared to QDR11,090,157 in 1971. Earnings on sterling assets were higher owing to the rise in interest rates in London in the second half of the year and to the increase in the board's sterling holdings, but low interest rates on Swiss franc and deutschmark deposits affected adversely earnings on these investments. In accordance with Article 34 of the Qatar-Dubai Currency Agreement the surplus of QDR10,141,862 was credited to the Special Reserve Account. Losses on revaluation of sterling assets, which were not included in the Currency Fund Income Account, were debited directly to the Special Reserve Account. They totalled QDR11,928,155 after deduction of QDR2,772,507 being compensation under the Sterling Guarantee Agreement received from the British Government.

These movements on the Special Reserve Account reduced the balance outstanding on that account from QDR17,459,753 as at the end of 1971 to QDR15,673,460 as at 31 December 1972. As at that date the balance on the Special Reserve Account represented 6.8 per cent of the currency in circulation. Under the circumstances no payment was made to the government of Qatar in respect of the operations of the year under review in accordance with the stipulations of Article 36 of the Qatar-Dubai Currency Agreement.

Appendix 5.4 Testing for Qatar-Dubai Currency Board Orthodoxy Authorised Currency Backing Analysis

	1966	1967	1968	1969	1970	1971	1972
1 Currency in circulation	85,466,306	130,632,973	146,547,259	152,897,514	152,097,531	174,597,531	232,097,559
Gold		23,160,021	30,833,513	30,833,513	30,833,513	30,833,513	30,833,513
British Government securities		27,884,285	28,348,214	45,438,035	31,255,892	14,627,321	13,181,329
Securities of Foreign Governments							
British Government Treasury Bills	26,888,566	73,041,974	51,313,046	47,363,313	55,014,021	96,868,311	136,935,041
Treasury Bills of Foreign Governments							
Cash with foreign banks on deposit and current account	58,760,269	6,632,267	42,795,477	43,616,360	58,836,434	56,737,196	60,397,705
1.1 Authorised Currency backing	85,648,835	130,718,547	153,290,250	167,251,221	175,939,860	199,066,341	241,347,588
1.2 Excess of Currency Backing over Currency in Circulation	182,529	85,574	6,742,991	14,353,707	23,842,329	24,468,810	9,250,029
Other net assets							
Cash with local banks		72,887	16,631	53,498	55,419	76,563	3,648,405
Plus Other net assets							
Interest due but not received	940,273	828,015	1,494,331	2,727,527	2,398,338	1,767,468	2,085,616
Fixed assets							
Sundry creditors							
1.3 Total of Excess backing and other net assets	1,122,802	986,476	8,253,953	17,134,732	26,296,086	26,312,841	14,984,050
Equals special reserve fund represented by:							
Special reserve account	101,790	979,229	8,250,855	15,289,751	15,209,753	17,459,753	15,673,459
1.4 Total capital and reserves	101,790	979229	8,250,855	15,289,751	15,209,753	17,459,753	15,673,459
		,					
(Qatar Dubai Riyals)							
Fiscal year ended 31st December							
	1966	**1967**	**1968**	**1969**	**1970**	**1971**	**1972**
Currency in circulation	85,446,306	130,632,973	146,547,259	152,897,514	152,097,531	174,597,531	232,097,559

AUTHORISED CURRENCY BACKING							
British Government Treasury Bills	26,888,566	73,041,974	51,313,046	47,363,313	55,014,021	96,868,311	136,935,041
Cash with foreign banks on deposit and current account	58,760,269	6,632,267	42,795,477	43,616,360	58,836,434	56,737,196	60,397,705
Gold		23,160,021	30,833,513	30,833,513	30,833,513	30,833,513	30,833,513
British Government securities		27,884,285	28,348,214	45,438,035	31,255,892	14,627,321	13,181,329
TOTAL AUTHORISED CURRENCY BACKING	85,648,835	130,718,547	153,290,250	167,251,221	175,939,860	199,066,341	241,347,588
1.5 Total assets	86,589,108	131,619,449	154,805,362	170,035,146	178,395,267	200,917,172	249,854,116
1.6 Total liabilities	86,487,308	130,640,223	146,554,509	154,745,396	163,185,516	183,457,421	234,180,659
Special reserve account	101,790	979,229	8,250,855	15,289,751	15,209,753	17,459,753	15,673,459
1.7 Total liabilities and reserve account	86,589,098	131,619,452	154,805,364	170,035,147	178,395,269	200,917,174	249,854,118
1.8 100% Orthodoxy Test	100.24	100.07	104.60	109.39	115.68	114.01	103.99
2.Tests for Currency Board Liquidity							
(Qatar Dubai Riyals)							
Fiscal Year Ended 31st December							
	1966	**1967**	**1968**	**1969**	**1970**	**1971**	**1972**
Currency in circulation	85,446,306	130,632,973	146,547,259	152,897,514	152,097,531	174,597,531	232,097,559
Liquid external assets							
British Government Treasury Bills	26,888,566	73,041,974	51,313,046	47,363,313	55,014,021	96,868,311	136,935,041
Cash with foreign banks on deposit and current account	58,760,269	6,632,267	42,795,477	43,616,360	58,836,434	56,737,196	60,397,705
Gold		23,160,021	30,833,513	30,833,513	30,833,513	30,833,513	30,833,513

2.1Total liquid external assets	**85,648,835**	**102,834,262**	**124,942,036**	**121,813,186**	**144,683,968**	**184,439,020**	**228,166,259**
2.2 Total liquid external assets as\a percentage of total external assets	100.00	78.67	81.51	72.83	82.23	92.65	94.54
Illiquid external assets							
British Government securities							
Total illiquid external assets		27,884,285	28,348,214	45,438,035	31,255,892	14,627,321	13,181,329
2.3 Total illiquid external assets as a percentage of total external assets	0.00	21.33	18.49	27.17	17.77	7.35	5.46
2.4 Total external assets	85,648,835	130,718,547	153,290,250	167,251,221	175,939,860	199,066,341	241,347,588
Total assets	86,589,108	131,619,449	154,805,362	170,035,146	178,395,267	200,917,172	249,854,116
Liabilities							
Total liabilities	86,487,308	130,640,223	146,554,509	154,745,396	163,185,516	183,457,421	234,180,659
Special reserve account	101,790	979,229	8,250,855	15,289,751	15,209,753	17,459,753	15,673,459
Total liabilities and reserve account	86,589,098	131,619,452	154,805,364	170,035,147	178,395,269	200,917,174	249,854,118
2.5 100 % Rule	100.237	100.066	104.601	109.388	115.676	114.014	103.985
6. Allocations to Government of Qatar-Dubai from Currency Board Income							
QATAR 1966-1972							
IMF data (International Financial Statistics) FOR CURRENCY BOARD PERIOD							

3. Tests of Currency Board Orthodoxy applying IMF data

Coverage of the monetary base by net foreign assets (end of period)

	1966	**1967**	**1968**	**1969**	**1970**	**1971**	**1972**
Foreign assets 11	34.3	52.3	65.4	75.5	84.7	94.30	125.90
Foreign liabilities	0	0	0	0	0	0	0
3.1 Net Foreign assets (NFA)	34.3	52.3	65.4	75.5	84.7	94.30	125.90
3.2 Reserve Money (MO)	34.2	52.3	58.6	61.2	60.8	69.80	92.80
3.3 Currency Outside Banks (COB's)		46.5	50.9	51.5	54.3	60.40	76.60
Coverage							
3.4 NFA/MO	100.29	100.00	111.60	123.37	139.31	135.10	135.67
3.5 NFA/COB's	138.87	112.47	128.49	146.60	155.99	156.13	164.36

Appendix 5.5

QATAR MONETARY AGENCY LAW 1973 – 1993

(A Monetary Agency and not a Currency Board)

1. The legal position of the Monetary Agency

Monetary Agency Law 1973.

2. Name of the central monetary institution

'There shall be established an Agency to be known as the Qatar Monetary Agency.'

3. Purposes of the Monetary Agency

'The purposes of the Agency shall be: (a) To regulate the issue, redemption and supply of currency; (b) to safeguard the internal and external value of the currency and its convertibility into other currencies; (c) to promote credit and exchange conditions conducive to the growth of the economy within the framework of monetary stability; and (d) to supervise the banks.'

4. Status of the Board of Directors

'The Board consists of a Governor, a Deputy Governor and five other Directors. Members are appointed by the Amir on the recommendation of the Minister responsible for Financial Affairs, the Governor and Deputy Governor for five-year terms, and the five other Directors for three-year terms. Appointments are renewable. The Governor and Deputy Governor must be full-time officers; the Governor is the chief executive and the Deputy Governor deputizes for him in his absence.'

5. Capital and ownership (summary of provisions)

'The capital of the Agency shall be ten million riyals and shall be paid by the Government in full upon the establishment of the Agency.'

6. Currency and external reserve requirements

'The unit of currency of Qatar shall be the riyal and shall be divided into one hundred dirhams.'

'The par value of the riyal and any change thereof shall be declared by an Amiri decree on the recommendation of the Agency and the approval of the Minister.'

'The value of the reserve of external assets provided for in paragraph (1) of this Article shall not be less than an amount equivalent to 100 per cent of the currency in circulation provided that the Board may, from time to time, with the approval of the Minister, alter the minimum reserve figures for periods not exceeding six months.'

Article 29 (1) specifies the permissible external reserve assets.

7. *Definition of 'bank' and 'banking business'*

"Bank' means any company licensed to carry on banking business in Qatar under Part IX of this Law.'

"Banking business' means the business of accepting from the public deposits repayable on demand or otherwise and withdraw able by cheques, draft, order or other means, for the purposes of extending credit or investment at the risk of the person accepting such deposit.'

8. *Head office, branches, agents and correspondents*

'The Agency shall have its Head Office in Doha and may, within Qatar or abroad: (a) establish and close branches; (b) appoint agents and correspondents and cancel such appointments.'

9. *The legal position of the Monetary Agency*

Monetary Agency Law 1973.

10. *Name of the central monetary institution*

'There shall be established an Agency to be known as the Qatar Monetary Agency.'

11. *Purposes of the Monetary Agency*

'The purposes of the Agency shall be: (a) To regulate the issue, redemption and supply of currency; (b) to safeguard the internal and external value of the currency and its convertibility into other currencies; (c) to promote credit and exchange conditions conducive to the growth of the economy within the framework of monetary stability; and (d) to supervise the banks.'

12. *Status of the Board of Directors*

'The Board consists of a Governor, a Deputy Governor and five other Directors. Members are appointed by the Amir on the recommendation of the Minister responsible for Financial Affairs, the Governor and Deputy Governor for five-year terms, and the five other Directors for three-year terms. Appointments are renewable. The Governor and Deputy Governor must be full-time officers; the Governor is the chief executive and the Deputy Governor deputizes for him in his absence.'

13. *Capital and ownership (summary of provisions)*

'The capital of the Agency shall be ten million riyals and shall be paid by the Government in full upon the establishment of the Agency.'

14. *Currency and external reserve requirements*

'The unit of currency of Qatar shall be the riyal and shall be divided into one hundred dirhams.'

'The par value of the riyal and any change thereof shall be declared by an Amiri decree on the recommendation of the Agency and the approval of the Minister.'

'The value of the reserve of external assets provided for in paragraph (1) of this Article shall not be less than an amount equivalent to 100 per cent of the currency in circulation provided that the Board may, from time to time, with the approval of the Minister, alter the minimum reserve figures for periods not exceeding six months.'

Article 29 (1) specifies the permissible external reserve assets.

15. *Definition of 'bank' and 'banking business'*

"Bank' means any company licensed to carry on banking business in Qatar under Part IX of this Law.'

"Banking business' means the business of accepting from the public deposits repayable on demand or otherwise and withdraw able by cheques, draft, order or other means, for the purposes of extending credit or investment at the risk of the person accepting such deposit.'

16. *Head office, branches, agents and correspondents*

'The Agency shall have its Head Office in Doha and may, within Qatar or abroad: (a) establish and close branches; (b) appoint agents and correspondents and cancel such appointments.'

Chapter 6

The Monetary and Banking Environment within Qatar 1965-1973 and its impact on Commercial Banking

The development of the banking and financial system in Qatar, as in many other states in the region, was greatly affected by the political and economic factors prevalent during Qatar's recent past.

In 1945 the country had no schools or telephones, and only one doctor to serve the estimated population of around 25,000, of whom about a fifth lived in the capital of Doha. During the 1950s and 1960s the economy grew as oil revenues poured in, although development was limited until the accession of Sheikh Khalifa bin Hamad in 1972.

By the mid-1970s Qatar had the second highest GNP per head in the world, exceeded only by Kuwait.

Politically, Qatar was under British influence until the early 1970s, as result of which it had economically all the features of the countries linked to the Sterling Area, the details of which were discussed in Chapter 3.

Currencies directly linked with the pound sterling, like the Indian rupee and then the Gulf rupee, were the currencies in circulation during that period. The pound sterling continued to provide the Qatari currency cover even after the issuance of the Qatar-Dubai riyal, which replaced the earlier currencies in 1966.

Under these circumstances, commercial banks of British origin were the pioneers in practising banking activities in Qatar.

The first such bank was a branch of the Eastern Bank, now known as Standard Chartered Bank. It was opened in 1950 after the commencement of production and the export of Qatari oil from early December 1949.

Banking activities remained a monopoly of the Eastern Bank until 1954 when the authorities felt the need to have another bank and consequently granted permission to the British Bank of the Middle East (BBME) to open a branch in the country. The first branch of BBME opened up in Doha, the capital city of Qatar, in March 1954. BBME expanded its activities as oil revenues grew. [1]

A third British bank, the Ottoman Bank, which later changed its name to Grindlays Bank, was permitted to open a branch in Qatar in 1965.

The steady increase in the production and export of Qatari oil in the subsequent years led to further expansion of the banking sector in order to keep pace with the growing economic activity.

Another bank, a branch of the Jordan based Arab Bank, was set up in 1975. A Lebanese bank later re-named Al Mashreq was also permitted to open a branch.

At the same time currency exchange activities started picking up momentum from the very early stage of development that corresponded with the then prevailing socio-economic circumstances.

In 1955 the first specialised exchange company, Al Fardan Jewellery Store, was established.

Until the mid-1960s Qatar remained dependent on foreign banks and still did not have its own national currency. The authorities, therefore, felt the need to remedy this situation.

In the banking sector, Qatar National Bank, the first Qatari bank, was established in 1965 as a result of government efforts. The bank was floated with a capital of 9 million Indian rupees shared equally between the government and the public and mandated to act as the government bank, a responsibility, until then, that had been entrusted to the Eastern Bank.

It was also due to the government's efforts that a currency agreement was concluded between Qatar and Dubai. It was signed on 21 March, 1966 after the failure in July of 1965 to conclude an agreement for a common Gulf currency between Qatar, Dubai, Abu Dhabi and Bahrain.

In accordance with the new agreement, the first national currency, known as the Qatar-Dubai riyal, was issued in the latter half of the same year to replace the many foreign currencies that were in circulation in the country at the time.

In the mid-1960s the pace of economic growth increased rapidly with the arrival of the Shell Oil Company in 1964. It joined hands with Qatar Petroleum Company which was, for nearly two decades, in charge of all production operations. With this development the scope of oil production and export expanded steadily and state revenues from oil increased substantially.

At the time developments in the Qatari economy led to a noticeable change in the size and composition of the country's financial structure.

During the period 1964-1970, growth in the foreign trade sector grew quickly. Five insurance companies were established with the Qatar Insurance Company taking the lead in 1964. Branches of three more foreign banks were also opened with a total capital of 15 million rupees shared equally between them.

Nine banks came into existence during the period including the Qatar National Bank. The assets and liabilities of these banks greatly increased during this period

At the dawn of independence on 3 September 1971 many changes were introduced internally and externally.

Within the country the government embarked on several measures designed to raise the level of socio-economic development. Externally it sought to become a member of all the key international organisations and agencies.

Among the major developments in the monetary and banking system was Qatar's membership of the International Monetary Fund., taking effect on 8 September 1972, just five days after independence.

Yet another important development was the approval, granted by the Ministry of Finance and Petroleum, to the agreement concluded by the Association of Commercial Banks operating in Qatar. This agreement, which aimed at regulating inter-bank operations with regard to interest rates on deposits and loans, was important at the time because of the absence of a national central monetary authority.

Due to political and functional considerations it became essential to establish a central monetary authority. After the merger of Dubai with the United Arab Emirates, a Law was issued on 19 May 1973, known as Law No. 7, announcing the establishment of the Qatar Monetary Agency (QMA thereafter). See Appendix 5.5 for the details.

The QMA assumed the duties of a central bank, including the issuance and regulation of the national currency in accordance with domestic economic needs. This included the maintenance of internal and external values of the national currency and its convertibility into other currencies, supervising the banking system and controlling domestic credit and other banking activities.

In order to appreciate the banking environment within which commercial banks evolved in Qatar , during the currency board period, it is essential to look at the monetary environment at that time period .

How do you Define and Measure the Banking and Monetary environment?

There are a series of key economic indicator classifications, in the context of Qatar, as applied by the IMF in their official publication, International Financial Statistics (IFS).[23]
These grouping criteria include:
1. Monetary Authorities
2. Commercial Banks
3. Monetary Survey
4. International Liquidity and Trade
5. Government Finance

1. Monetary Authorities

The Monetary Authorities' data measure the creation of reserve money comprising currency in circulation and the deposits of the deposit money banks and the demand deposits of the private sector with the monetary authorities. Monetary authorities are broken down , in IFS, into Foreign Assets and Reserve Money, which is further subdivided into Currency outside banks. The data focus on the economic sector classification of assets and liabilities with the latter further classified by the degree of liquidity.

On the asset side, foreign assets are shown gross to highlight the function of the monetary authorities as the holder of international reserves and other foreign claims. Domestic assets are classified as claims on government; claims on deposit money banks and, if sizeable, claims on official entities and the private sector.

The principal liabilities consist of reserve money, foreign liabilities, and government deposits.

Monetary authorities' data, in IFS , consolidate the accounts of the currency board with the accounts arising from the standard monetary functions of the government, such as the issuance of currency or the holding of international reserves and positions vis-à-vis the IMF.

Foreign assets are financial claims on non-residents, regardless of the denomination of the financial instrument. Foreign assets thus include holdings of cash issued by non-resident central banks and other claims on non-residents. Holdings of monetary gold and Special Drawing Rights are also included under claims on non-residents.

The foreign assets holdings of the Qatar monetary authorities grew from QDR210.2m in 1965 to QDR319.2m in 1973. A 52 per cent growth rate, in line with the growing economy. See Figure 6.1.

Foreign liabilities consist of indebtedness to non-residents. Strictly speaking equity liabilities (e.g. shares) held by non-residents should also be included under foreign liabilities. Given that there were no foreign liabilities during this time period then the foreign assets figure was identical to the net foreign assets.

An important monetary aggregate is reserve money (M0) which is the monetary base. As reserve money grows so do deposits in deposit money banks and with it the monetary aggregates.

Reserve Money consists of the monetary authorities' liabilities in the form of:
1. Currency in circulation outside the monetary authorities
2. Bankers reserves (deposit money banks domestic cash in vaults plus their required and free deposits with the central bank or similar institution)
3. Demand deposits of the rest of the domestic economy (excluding banks and central government, the latter normally being a small amount)

Reserve Money grew rapidly from QDR34.2m in 1965 to QDR92.8m in 1973, a growth rate of some 170 per cent, again in line with economic growth. Data for reserve money and currency outside banks are given in Figure 6.2.

Currency held outside Deposit Money Banks (DMBs) is that part of reserve money held by the non-bank public. In IFS this is an item under Reserve Money. While currency outside banks is shown, all currency issued by the monetary authority is included in reserve money, including currency held by banks.

Currency held outside deposit money banks is defined as notes and coins accepted as legal tender in the domestic economy, excluding amounts held by the monetary system, central government and non-residents.

So, currency held outside DMBs is currency held by the public. Banks also hold some currency as vault cash for depositors seeking to withdraw cash.

Within the Reserve Money component, the currency held outside DMBs also grew rapidly from QDR24.7m in 1965 to QDR76.2m in 1973, a 208 per cent growth rate. Data for reserve money and currency outside deposit money banks are given in Figure 6.2.

What is the reason for the distinction between IFS Reserve Money and Currency held outside Deposit Money Banks?

The deposits of the monetary system (banks), central government, and non-residents are typically not included in the IMF money aggregates. Thus, for deriving money multipliers (broad money/money in circulation outside banks), their holdings of currency are excluded for consistency of numerator and denominator. The broader point here is that banks are part of the money issuing sector (in that they 'issue' deposits).

Accordingly, any deposits of banks with the central bank or any holdings of local currency are excluded from the monetary aggregates to provide a measure of money balances held by the non-money issuing (private) sector. In practice, only data on holdings of currency by banks (till money), and sometimes holdings by central government, are available and therefore excluded. It is difficult to generalise about the size of currency holdings by banks and central government, but one would not expect it to be large in an efficient and well-functioning financial system.

The rapid growth of Reserve Money and Foreign Assets and liabilities, during the period, is highlighted in Figure 6.1.

As can be seen from Figure 6.1, foreign assets grew from QDR34.3m in 1966 to QDR125.9m in 1972, a growth rate of 268 per cent. Reserve money grew from QDR34.2m in 1966 to QDR92.8m in 1972, a growth rate of 117 per cent. Government deposits grew from QDR1m in 1972 to QDR23.8m in 1972 , a growth rate of 228 per cent.

Figure 6.1 Monetary Authorities: Foreign Assets, Reserve Money and Government Deposits 1966-1972

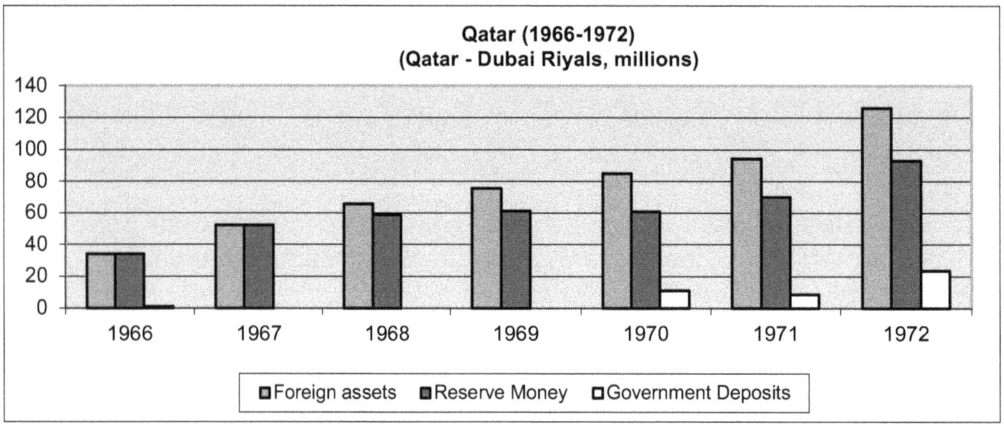

Source: International Financial Statistics, IMF

Figure 6.2 shows that Reserve Money grew from QDR34.2m in 1966 to QDR92.8m in 1972, a growth rate of 171 per cent. The currency outside banks component grew from QDR24.7m in 1966 to QDR76.6m in 1972, a growth rate of 210 per cent .

Figure 6.2 Monetary Authorities: Reserve Money and Currency outside Banks 1966-1972

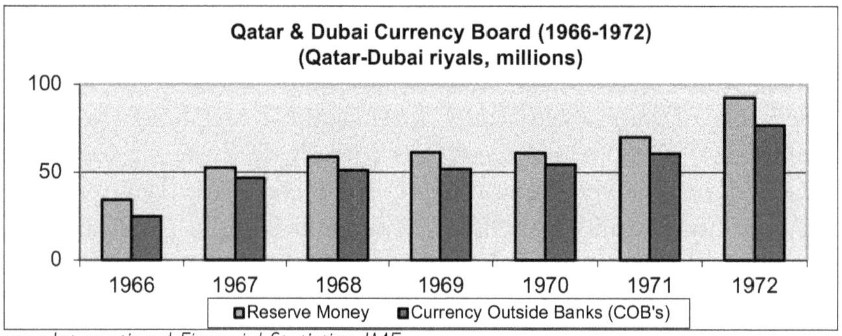

Source: International Financial Statistics, IMF

2. Commercial Banks

As can be seen from Figure 6.3 commercial bank assets grew from QDR48m in 1966 to QDR73m in 1972, a 52 per cent growth rate. Liability growth was substantially lower than asset growth.

Deposit Money Banks include currency boards, which have significant liabilities in the form of deposits payable on demand and transferable by cheque or otherwise usable in making payments. Deposit money banks comprise commercial banks and other banks that have demand deposits.

The deposit money banks data measures the creation of deposit money. Major aggregates of the accounts are reserves, comprising currency holdings and deposits with monetary authorities, claims on the private sector, demand deposits and time and savings deposits.

Generally reserve money minus currency outside banks is approximately equal to deposit money bank reserves.

Data for commercial banks foreign assets and liabilities and claims on the private sector are given in Figure 6.4 which highlights that this was clearly a period of rapid growth in these monetary aggregates.

Appendix 6.1 provides consolidated balance sheets for banks in Qatar for the period 1965-1972.

Figure 6.3 Commercial Bank Assets 1966-1972

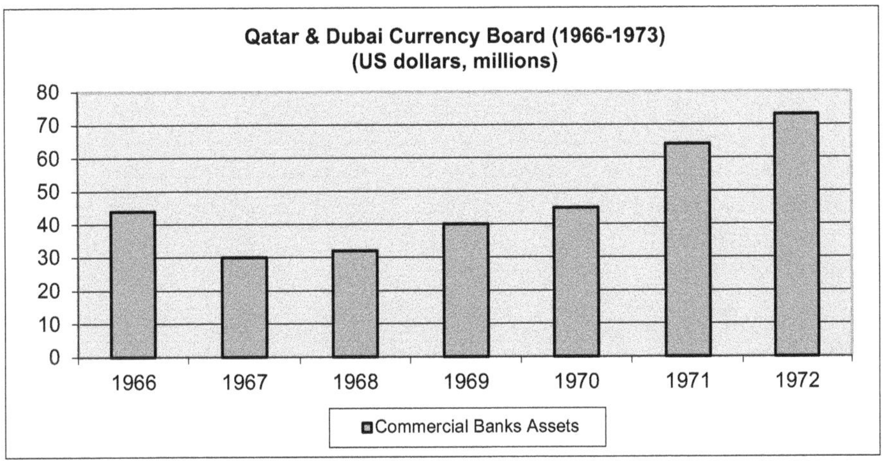

Source: International Financial Statistics, IMF

Figure 6.4 highlights that commercial banks foreign assets grew from QDR210.2m in 1966 to QDR319.8m in 1972, a 62 per cent growth rate. At the same time foreign liabilities fell from QDR14.9m in 1966 to QDR2.5m in 1972.

Figure 6.4 Commercial Banks: Foreign assets and Liabilities 1966-1972

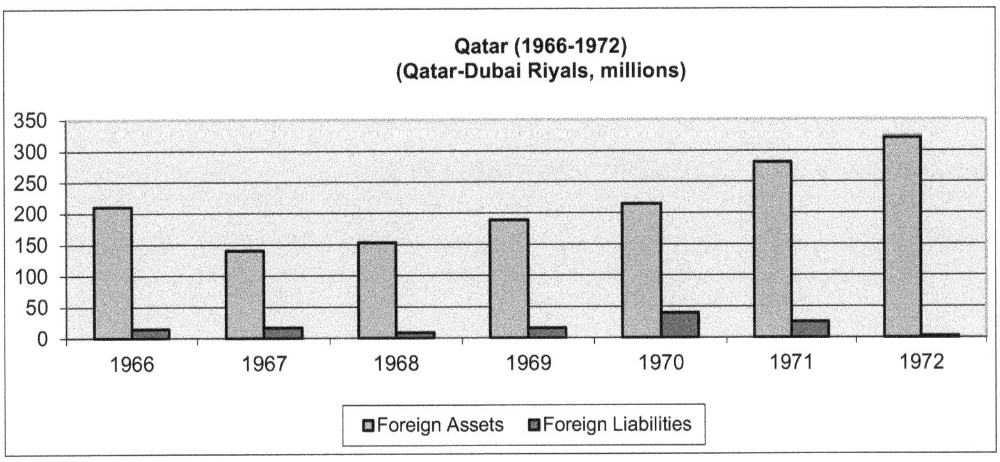

Source: International Financial Statistics, IMF

Figure 6.5 highlights that commercial bank reserves grew from QDR9.5m in 1966 to QDR16.5m in !972, a 73 per cent growth rate. Claims on the private sector grew from QDR103m to QDR332m in 1972, a growth rate of 221 per cent . Demand deposits grew from QDR92.5m in 1966 to QDR268.8m in 1972, a 190 per cent growth rate . At the same time Time and Saving deposits grew from QDR120m to QDR318m in 1972, a growth rate of 165 per cent. Business was booming.

Figure 6.5 Commercial Banks: Reserves, Claims on Private Sector, Demand and Time and Saving Deposits 1966-1972

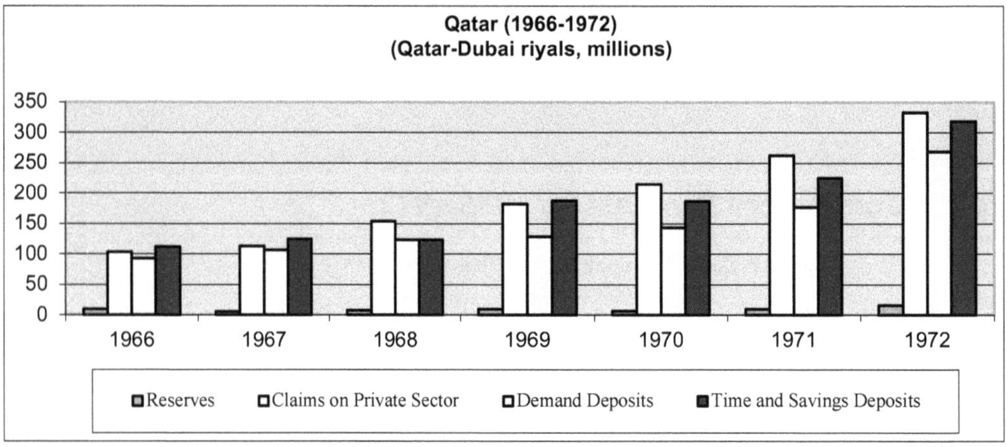

Source: International Financial Statistics, IMF

3. Monetary Survey

Monetary authority and deposit money bank data are consolidated by the IMF into what is called the Monetary Survey in order to measure the size and origin of money and quasi-money.

Money is defined as M1 - currency held by the public and demand deposits. Quasi-money is time deposits, savings deposits and foreign currency deposits. Data for money and quasi-money are given in Figure 6.6.

Money grew rapidly from QDR117.2m in 1965 to QDR345.5m in 1972, a 194 per cent growth. Quasi-money also grew substantially from QDR111.9m in 1965 to QDR318.6m in 1972, a growth rate of 184 per cent. Claims on the private sector grew very rapidly from QDR103m in 1965 to QDR332.7m in 1972, a growth rate of 223 per cent. Clearly the economy was booming as was the growth of commercial banking.

Figure 6.6 Money and Quasi-Money 1966-1972

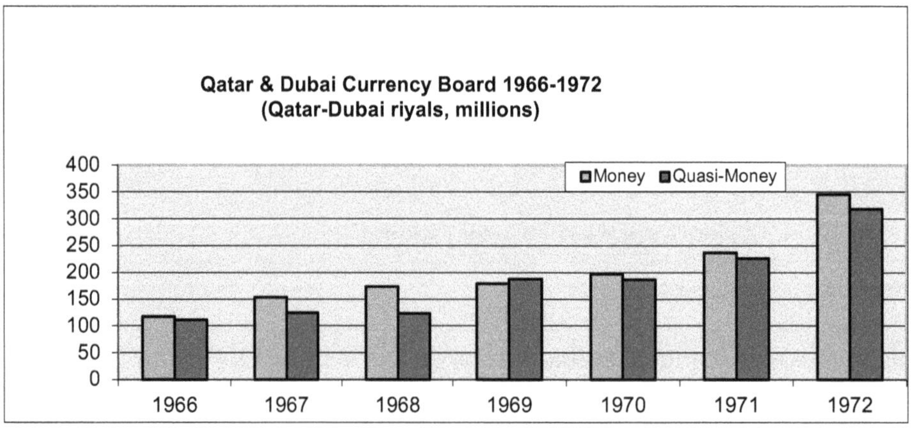

Source: International Financial Statistics, IMF

Figure 6.7 consolidates the accounts foreign assets, claims on the private sector, money and quasi-money. They all grew substantially between 1966 and 1972.

Figure 6.7 Monetary Survey: Foreign Assets, Claims on Private Sector, Money and Quasi-Money 1966-1972

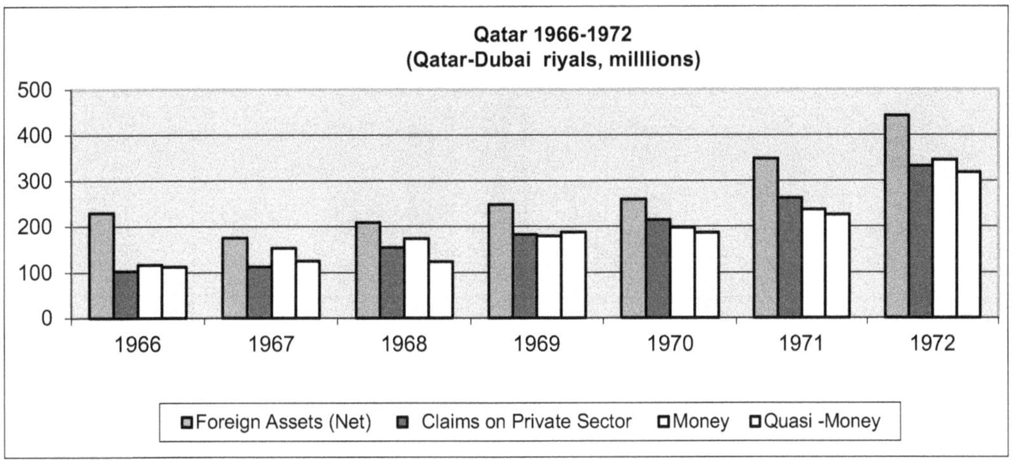

Source: International Financial Statistics, IMF

4. International Trade and International Liquidity

The relevant IFS country pages report the value for Qatar gold holdings, the reserve position in the IMF, their foreign exchange and the sum of these items, total reserves minus gold. See Figure 6.8.

Foreign exchange includes monetary authority claims on non-residents in the form of bank deposits, treasury bills, short-term and long-term government securities, and other claims usable in the event of a balance of payments deficit.

These include non-marketable claims arising from inter central bank and intergovernmental arrangements, without regard to whether the claim is denominated in the currency of the debtor or the creditor.

The foreign accounts of financial institutions, other than the monetary authorities, are also reported in the international liquidity section of the IFS country pages.

During the period under consideration Qatari gold holdings remained between 0.14 and 0.19 million fine troy ounces whilst their monetary valuation rose from $US4.9m in 1966 to $US7.0m in 1973.

The IMF Reserve Position stood at $US 5.4m in 1972. Total reserves minus gold holdings rose rapidly from $US7.2m in 1966 to $US21.6m in 1973. A growth rate of 202 per cent. Data for International Liquidity are given in Figure 6.8

The data for total reserves minus gold holdings can be regarded as being the international liquidity holdings of Qatar.

The principal source of international liquidity can be seen as almost exclusively that of the growth in foreign exchange holdings. These grew from $US9.2m in 1966 to $US60.2m in 1973. They grew by some 550 per cent. Again evidence of a booming economy.

Figure 6.8 International Liquidity 1965-1973 ($US millions)

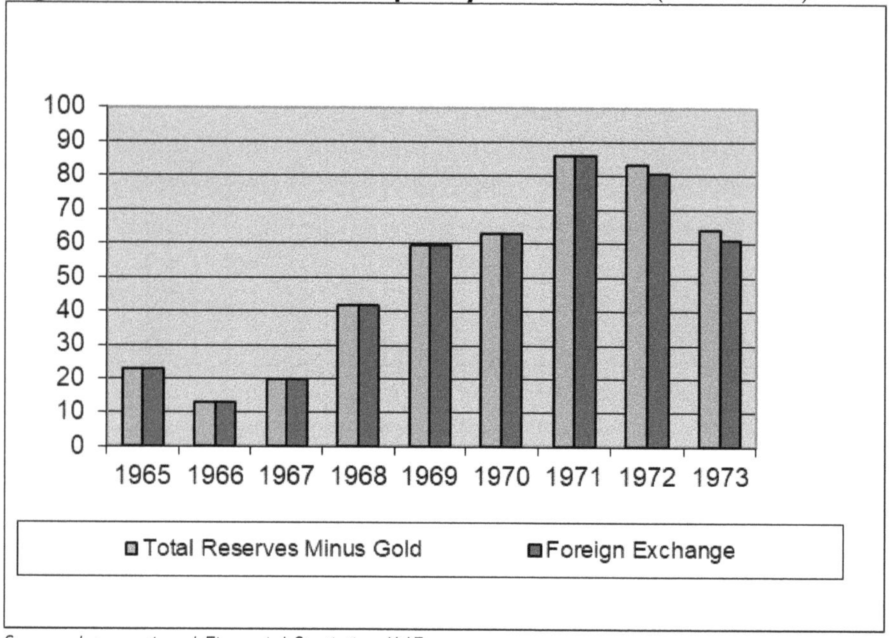

Source: International Financial Statistics, IMF

As can be seen from Figure 6.9, exports grew from QDR850m in 1966 to QDR1,740m in 1972, a growth rate of 104 per cent. At the same time imports grew from QDR252m in 1969 to QDR616m in 1972, a growth rate of 144 per cent.

Figure 6.9 Foreign Trade

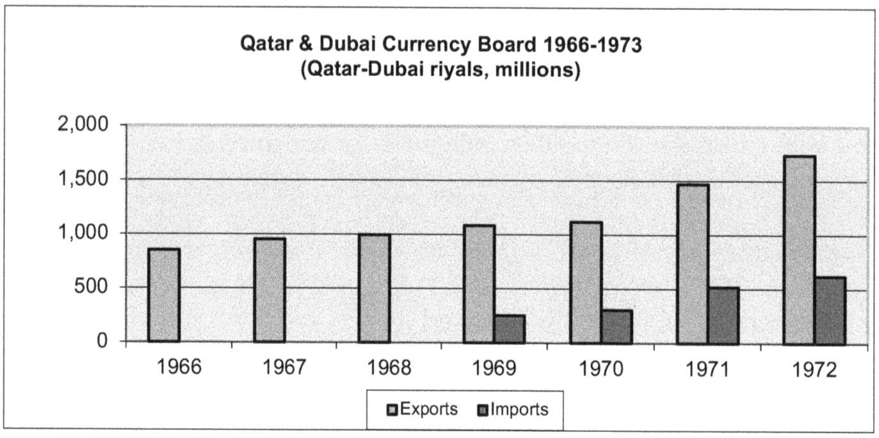

Source: International Financial Statistics, IMF

Government Finance

The Qatar government ran surpluses for the period. Both revenues and expenditure rose rapidly during the period for which data is available,1970-1972. Revenue rose from QDR579.4m in 1970 reaching QDR1,230m by 1972, a growth rate of 112 per cent. Expenditure, which grew less rapidly than revenues grew from QDR504.6m in 1970 to QDR958.6m by 1972, a growth rate of 90 per cent.

Data for government finance and the government fiscal position are given in Figure 6.10. As can be seen from Figure 6.10 government revenue and expenditure grew rapidly between 1970 and 1972.

Figure 6.10 Government Finance

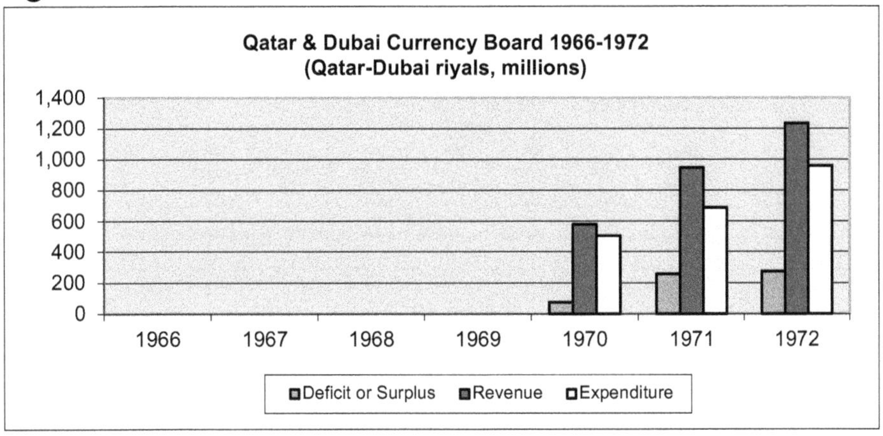

Source: International Financial Statistics, IMF

REFERENCES

[1] Jones G. *Banking and Oil: The History of the British Bank of the Middle East. Vol. 2.* Cambridge University Press, Cambridge 1987

[2] *IMF Monetary and Financial Statistics Manual,* pp325-330 2000

[3] *IMF System of National Accounts. IMF Balance of Payments Manual (Fifth edition)* 1993

El Mallakh, Ragaei. *Qatar: Development of an Oil Economy.* Croom Helm, London and St Martin's Press, New York 1979

El Mallakh, Ragaei. *Qatar: Energy and Development.* Croom Helm, London 1985

Nafi, Zuhair Ahmed. *Economic and Social Development in Qatar.* Frances Pinter, London and Dover, New Hampshire 1983

Sadik, Muhammed T. and William P. Snavely. *Bahrain, Qatar and the UAE.* D.C. Heath and Company, Lexington, Mass. 1972

The Banking and Financial System in Qatar. Qatar Monetary Agency, December 1992.

Annual Reports. Qatar Dubai Currency Board for period ended 31 December 1966, 1967, 1968, 1969, 1970, 1971. See Appendix 5.4

Annual Report. Qatar-Dubai Currency Board for period ended 31 December 1972

Graham, Helga. *Arabian Time Machine: Self-Portrait of an Oil State.* Heinemann, London 1978

Al-Othman, Nasser. *With Their Bare Hands: The Story of the Oil Industry in Qatar.* Longman, London and New York 1984

APPENDIX I Currency Arrangements in the Gulf States prior to the formation of Central Banks

Country	Date of Creation of Currency (Name of Currency)	Name of Currency Withdrawn	Currency Board Dates	Currency Board Name	Date of Independence of Central Bank
Oman	7 May 1970 (Saidi rial) November 1972 (Omani rial)	Gulf rupee Saidi rial	(1) 1970-1972 (2) 1972-1974	Muscat Currency Authority Oman Currency Board	December 1974
United Arab Emirates	20 May 1973 (UAE dirham)	(1) Bahraini dinar (2) Qatar & Dubai riyal	1966–1973	Qatar & Dubai Currency Board	December 1980
Qatar	18 September 1966 (Qatar & Dubai riyal)	Saudi riyal	(1) 1966-1973 (2) 1973-1993	Qatar/Dubai Currency Board Qatar Monetary Agency	1993
Bahrain	16 October 1965 (Bahraini dinar)	Gulf rupee	1965–1973	Bahrain Currency Board	1973
Kuwait	October 1960 (Kuwaiti dinar)	Gulf rupee	1961–1969	Kuwait Currency Board	1968
Libya	June 1952 (Libyan pound)	(1) Egyptian Pound Military Authority lire (2) Algerian franc	1952–1956	Libyan Currency Commission	April 1955
Iraq	June 1932 (Iraqi dinar)	Indian rupee	1931–1949	Iraq Currency Board	16 November 1947
Transjordan	1950 (Jordanian dinar)	Palestine pound	1950–1964	Jordan Currency Board	10 October 1964
Yemen	April 1965 (Yemeni Dinar)	East African Shilling	1964 – 1971	Yemen Currency Board	1971

Appendix 2 Currency Arrangements in the Middle East prior to the creation of Central Banks

Country (current name) [colonial power], year independent	Years	Reserve ratio and assets	Currency System	Exchange rate, exchange spread permitted
Abu Dhabi [UK] 1971	1966-1973	100+% gold and foreign exchange	Bahraini Dinar Peg	1 Bahrain dinar = 17s. 6d. sterling
Aden [UK], 1967	1951-1965	100% sterling	Member of East African Currency Board	20 East African Shillings = £1 sterling +1/2% 1942-1965;
Aden Protectorate (part of Yemen) [UK], 1967	1965-1972	100+% sterling after first 2.5 million dinars	South Arabian Currency Board	South Arabian/South Yemen dinar = £1 Sterling +3/4%
Yemen Arab Republic (part of Yemen)	1964-1971	100%,+ sterling	South Arabian Currency Board	3 Yemen rials = £1 sterling
Bahrain [UK], 1971	1965-1973	100+% foreign exchange	Bahrain Currency Board	1 Bahrain dinar = 17s. 6d. sterling
Dubai and Qatar [UK] 1971	1966-1973	100% gold and foreign exchange	Qatar and Dubai Currency Board	1 Qatar/Dubai riyal = 0.16621g gold
Iraq [UK], 1932	1931-1949	100%+% sterling	Iraq Currency Board	1 Iraqi dinar = £1 sterling , +1/2%?
Kuwait [UK], 1961	1961-1969	Min. 50% gold + max. 50% US$ sterling = 100%	Kuwait Currency Board	1 Kuwaiti dinar = £1 sterling
Libya [UK, France], 1951	1952-1956	100% sterling	Libyan Currency Board	Libyan £1 = £1 sterling , +1/4%
Oman	1970-1974	100+% sterling	Oman Currency Board	1 rial Omani = £1 sterling s
Palestine (Israel) [UK], 1948	1917-1948 (1926-1951 in Gaza	110% sterling	Palestine Currency Board	Palestine £1 = £1 sterling , +1/8%

Country (current name) [colonial power], year independent	Years	Reserve ratio and assets	Currency System	Exchange rate, exchange spread permitted
	Strip)			
Transjordan (Jordan) [UK], 1946	1927-1964	110% sterling	Jordan Currency Board	Palestine £1 = £1 sterling , +1/8% 1917-1948; 1 Jordanian dinar = £1 Sterling , +1/8% 1948- 1964

Appendix 3 From Currency Board (Monetary Agency) to IMF Membership: The Gulf States

. Country	Currency Board Dates (1)	. Currency Board Name	Date of Independence of Central Bank (Monetary Agency)	Central Bank (Monetary Agency) Name	Date of Sovereign Independence (Colonial Power)	Date of IMF Membership	Earliest date IMF monetary & currency data available
. . Oman(1) (2)	. 1970–1972 1972-1974	. Muscat Currency Authority Oman Currency Board	. December 1974	. Central Bank of Oman	. 9/10/1970 (UK)	. 23/12/1971	. 1970
United Arab Emirates	Dec 1974 –Dec 1980	United Arab Emirates Currency Board	December 1980	Central Bank of the UAE	2/12/1971 (UK)	22/09/1972	1973
Qatar(1)	Dec 1966 – Dec 1972	Qatar and Dubai Currency Board	1973 . 1993	Qatar Monetary Agency Qatar Central Bank	03/09/1971 (UK)	08/09/1972	1966
Bahrain	1965–1973	Bahrain Currency Board	1973	Bahrain Monetary Agency	15/08/1971 (UK)	07/09/1972	1965
Kuwait	1961–1969	Kuwait Currency Board	. 1968	Central Bank of Kuwait	19/06/1961 (UK)	13/09/1962	1949
Saudi Arabia [2]			1952	Saudi Arabian Monetary Agency	.	. 26/08/1957	. 1961

[1] As reported in Annual report

[2] Not a Currency Board Country

Appendix 4 From Currency Board (Currency Commission) to IMF Membership: The Middle East (excluding the Gulf States)

Country	Currency Board Dates (1)	Currency Board Name	Date of Independence of Central Bank (Monetary Agency)	Central Bank Name	Date of Sovereign Independence (Colonial Power)	Date of IMF Membership	Earliest date IMF data available
Libya	1952–1956	Libyan Currency Commission	April 1955	Central Bank of Libya	1951 (UK, France)	17/09/1958	1958
Iraq	1931–1949	Iraq Currency Board	16/09/1947	Central Bank of Iraq	British Mandate 14/7/1958 Republic of Iraq (UK)	27/12/1945	1949
Trans (Jordan)	1950–1964	Jordan Currency Board	10/10/1964	Central Bank of Jordan	25/5/1946 (UK)	29/08/1952	1951
Palestine	1926–1952 1948–1951	Palestine Currency Board		Palestine Monetary Authority [2]			
Israel			1954	Bank of Israel	14/5/1948	12/7/1954	1953
Aden Protectorate (part of Yemen)	1964 – 1971	Yemen Currency Board	1971	Central Bank of Yemen	1971 (UK)	22/05/1970	1972

[1] As reported in Annual reports.
[2] Central bank status not widely recognised.

www.ingramcontent.com/pod-product-compliance
Ingram Content Group UK Ltd.
Pitfield, Milton Keynes, MK11 3LW, UK
UKHW052302280926
15471UKWH00007B/1059

9 781739 800406